AN INSIDE LOOK

THE WORLD OF

ANIMAL LIFE

Please visit our web site at: www.garethstevens.com
For a free color catalog describing Gareth Stevens Publishing's
list of high-quality books and multimedia programs,
call 1-800-542-2595 (USA) or 1-800-461-9120 (Canada).
Gareth Stevens Publishing's Fax: (414) 332-3567.

The editors would like to thank Jan Rafert of the Milwaukee County
Zoo, Milwaukee, Wisconsin, for his kind and professional help with
the information in this book.

Library of Congress Cataloging-in-Publication Data

Legg, Gerald.
    The world of animal life / text by Gerald Legg; illustrated by Steve Weston.
        p. cm. — (An Inside look)
    Includes bibliographical references and index.
    ISBN 0-8368-2902-6 (lib. bdg.)
    1. Animals—Juvenile literature. 2. Anatomy—Juvenile literature.
  [1. Animals.] I. Weston, Steve, ill. II. Title. III. Series.
  QL49.L3728   2001
  590—dc21   2001020154

This North American edition first published in 2001 by
Gareth Stevens Publishing
A World Almanac Education Group Company
330 West Olive Street, Suite 100
Milwaukee, WI 53212 USA

This U.S. edition © 2001 by Gareth Stevens, Inc. Original
edition © 1998 by Horus Editions Limited. First published
as *The World of Animal Life* in the series *How It Works* by Horus
Editions Limited, 1st Floor, 27 Longford Street, London
NW1 3DZ, United Kingdom. Additional end matter © 2001
by Gareth Stevens, Inc.

Illustrators: Steve Weston, Ruth Lindsay, and David Wright
Gareth Stevens designer: Scott M. Krall
Gareth Stevens editors: Katherine J. Meitner and Alan Wachtel

Printed in the United States of America

1 2 3 4 5 6 7 8 9 05 04 03 02 01

AN INSIDE LOOK

THE
WORLD OF
ANIMAL LIFE

Gerald Legg

Gareth Stevens Publishing
A WORLD ALMANAC EDUCATION GROUP COMPANY

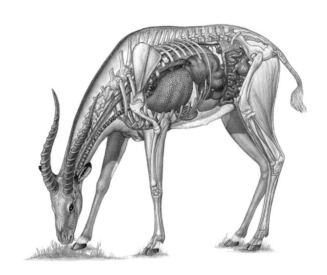

AN INSIDE LOOK

CONTENTS

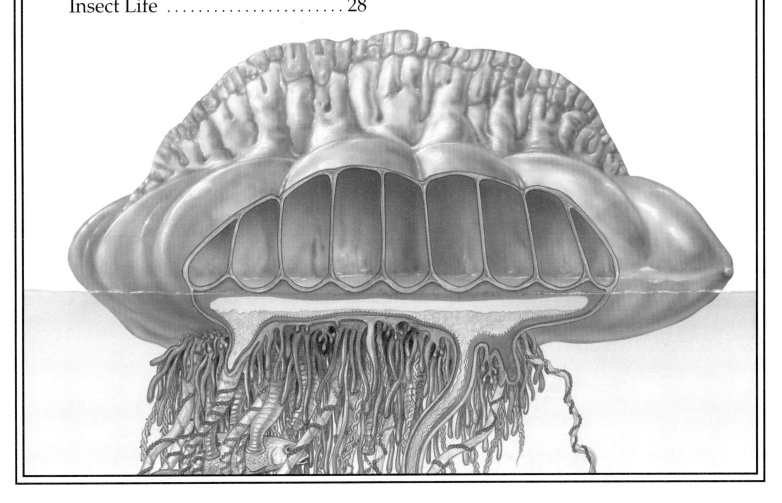

Bony Fish

The Anthias is a colorful fish that has a skeleton made of bones. About 20,000 different kinds of fish have bony skeletons. Its skeleton gives a fish its shape. Its shape allows it to move and act in certain ways.

Many fish are shaped so they can move quickly through water. Most fish have a long body that is pointed at the head and becomes narrow at the tail. Not all fish, however, are streamlined this way. Some fish that live among coral or seaweed or on the ocean floor move differently, so they need different body shapes.

Bony skeletons help fish eat, whether they hunt or scavenge for food. When it's ready to eat, a bony fish simply gets close to its meal and opens its mouth. The opening of the jaw bones around the mouth and gills opens up the throat. Water then rushes into the mouth, bringing the food with it.

EEL

FLYING FISH

ANGEL FISH

SEAHORSE

BONY FIN RAYS SPREAD ACROSS THE TAIL FIN, GIVING IT STRENGTH.

TAIL FIN

WITH SUDDEN MOVEMENTS OF ITS POWERFUL TAIL, A FISH CAN QUICKLY INCREASE ITS SPEED TO CATCH FOOD OR ESCAPE AN ENEMY.

SCALE

ANAL FIN

PECTORAL FIN

MUSCLE

EPIDERMIS (SKIN)

AS THE SCALES GROW, RINGS ARE PRODUCED. THE NUMBER OF RINGS ON THE SCALES INDICATES THE AGE OF THE FISH.

Fins

Fish use their fins in all kinds of ways. Eels have a long dorsal fin that ripples, gently propelling them along the ocean bottom. Flying fish have big winglike pectoral fins on their chests. The fins of angel fish allow them to make sharp turns through coral reefs. Seahorses have a dorsal fin on their backs that enables them to hover and move delicately through seaweed.

PELVIC AND PECTORAL FINS STEER THE FISH, MOVE IT UP AND DOWN IN THE WATER, AND ACT AS BRAKES.

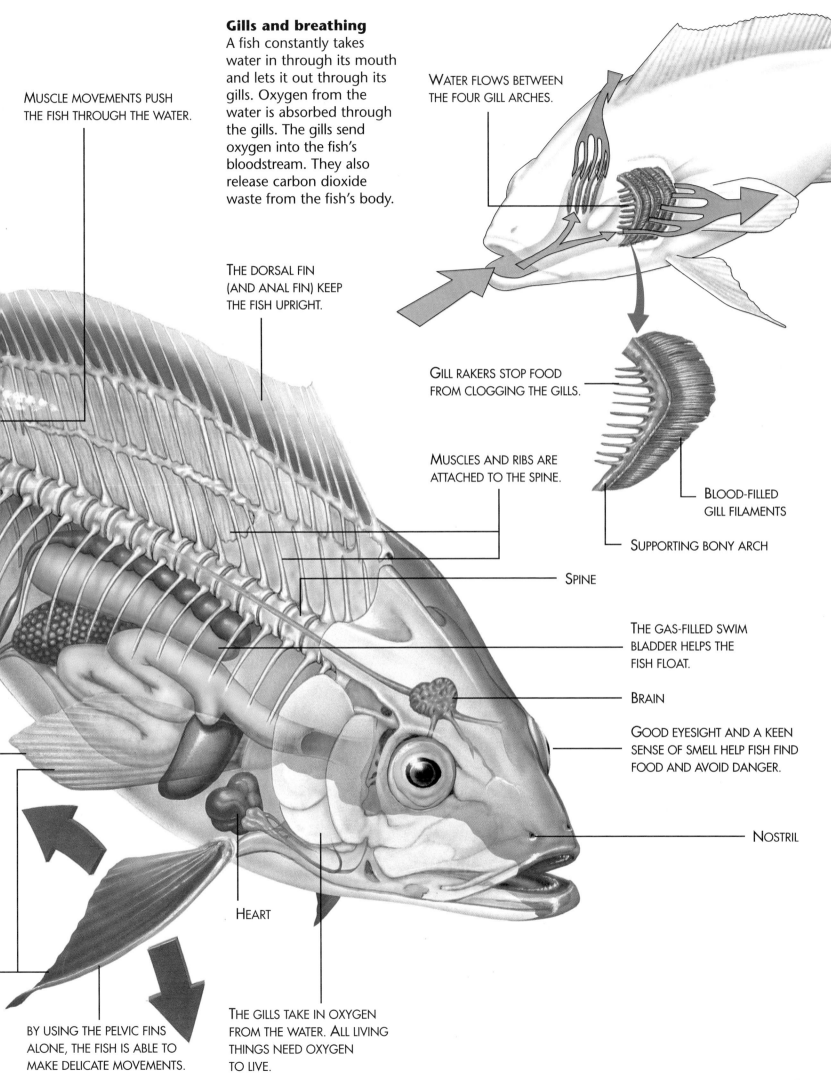

Gills and breathing
A fish constantly takes water in through its mouth and lets it out through its gills. Oxygen from the water is absorbed through the gills. The gills send oxygen into the fish's bloodstream. They also release carbon dioxide waste from the fish's body.

MUSCLE MOVEMENTS PUSH THE FISH THROUGH THE WATER.

WATER FLOWS BETWEEN THE FOUR GILL ARCHES.

THE DORSAL FIN (AND ANAL FIN) KEEP THE FISH UPRIGHT.

GILL RAKERS STOP FOOD FROM CLOGGING THE GILLS.

MUSCLES AND RIBS ARE ATTACHED TO THE SPINE.

BLOOD-FILLED GILL FILAMENTS

SUPPORTING BONY ARCH

SPINE

THE GAS-FILLED SWIM BLADDER HELPS THE FISH FLOAT.

BRAIN

GOOD EYESIGHT AND A KEEN SENSE OF SMELL HELP FISH FIND FOOD AND AVOID DANGER.

NOSTRIL

HEART

BY USING THE PELVIC FINS ALONE, THE FISH IS ABLE TO MAKE DELICATE MOVEMENTS.

THE GILLS TAKE IN OXYGEN FROM THE WATER. ALL LIVING THINGS NEED OXYGEN TO LIVE.

Bird Flight

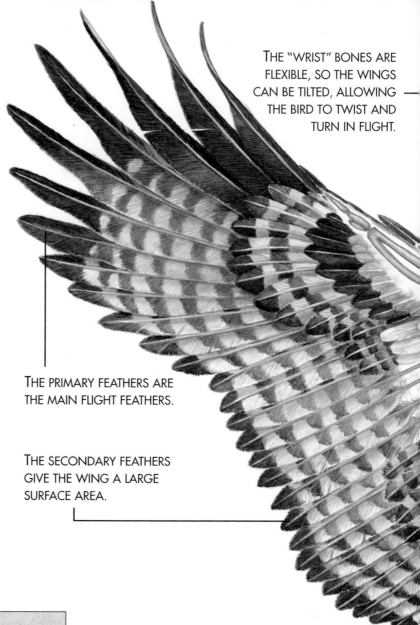

THE "WRIST" BONES ARE FLEXIBLE, SO THE WINGS CAN BE TILTED, ALLOWING THE BIRD TO TWIST AND TURN IN FLIGHT.

The osprey is a bird of prey. It flies over rivers, lakes, and seas, hunting for fish. When it spots a fish, the osprey dives feet-first into the water. Then, after grabbing its prey, the hawklike bird soars back up into the sky.

Like all birds, the osprey must flap its wings downward against the air to push its body upward. A bird's wings are airfoils, having the special curved shape that produces lift. This force keeps the bird in the air. The wing's shape also allows the bird to glide or soar on currents of air. For example, birds hardly need to flap their wings at all if they can "ride" on a wind that carries them upward over a hill. To steer, birds change the angle of their wings or twist their tails like rudders.

THE PRIMARY FEATHERS ARE THE MAIN FLIGHT FEATHERS.

THE SECONDARY FEATHERS GIVE THE WING A LARGE SURFACE AREA.

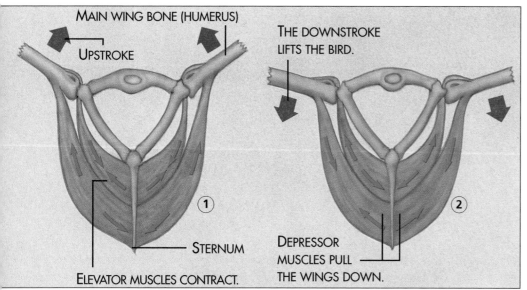

MAIN WING BONE (HUMERUS)

UPSTROKE

THE DOWNSTROKE LIFTS THE BIRD.

① ②

STERNUM

ELEVATOR MUSCLES CONTRACT.

DEPRESSOR MUSCLES PULL THE WINGS DOWN.

BROAD TAIL FEATHERS ACT LIKE A RUDDER FOR STEERING.

THE SHARP, CLAWED TOES ARE CALLED TALONS.

Flapping the wings

To fly through the air or hover, a bird must beat its wings. A pair of large breast muscles allow each wing to move. For an upward stroke (1), the depressor muscles relax and lengthen, and the elevator muscles contract and shorten. This motion lifts the wing bones like a pulley. For the downward stroke (2), which lifts the bird, the bigger, stronger depressor muscles must contract to pull the wing bones down.

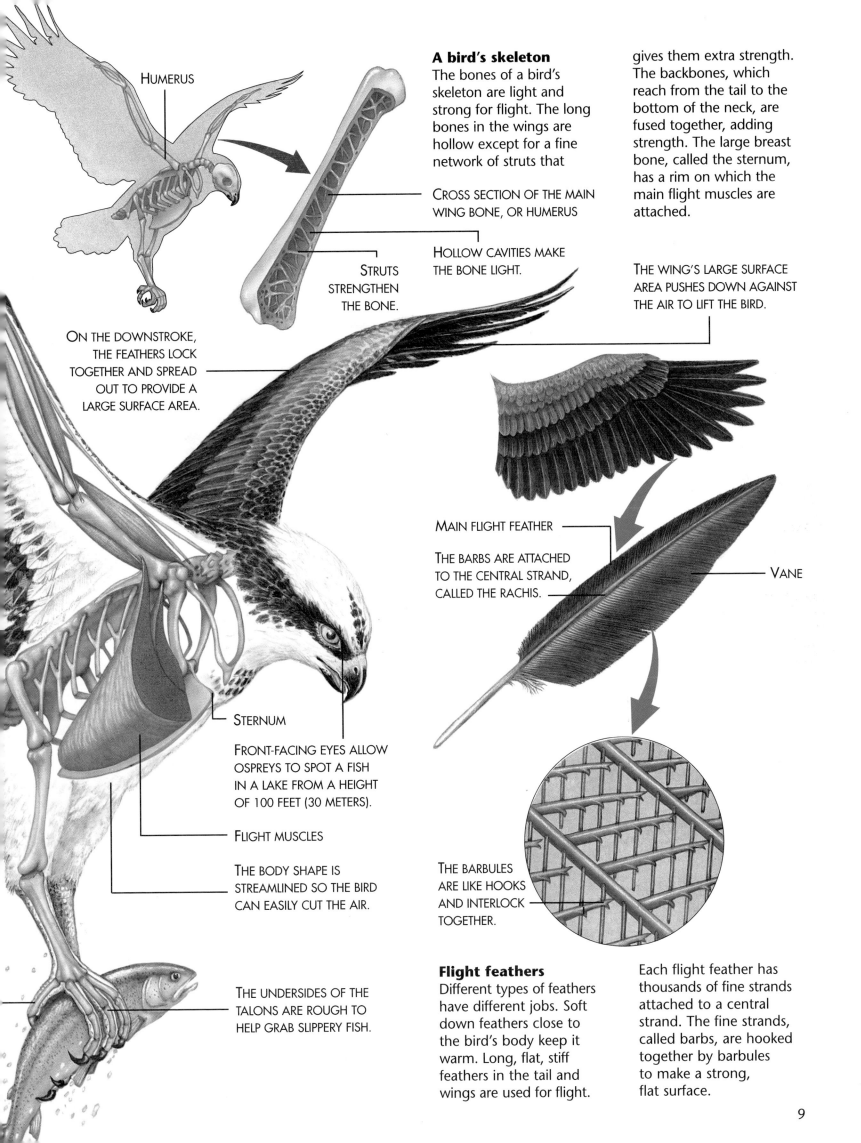

HUMERUS

CROSS SECTION OF THE MAIN WING BONE, OR HUMERUS

STRUTS STRENGTHEN THE BONE.

HOLLOW CAVITIES MAKE THE BONE LIGHT.

A bird's skeleton
The bones of a bird's skeleton are light and strong for flight. The long bones in the wings are hollow except for a fine network of struts that gives them extra strength. The backbones, which reach from the tail to the bottom of the neck, are fused together, adding strength. The large breast bone, called the sternum, has a rim on which the main flight muscles are attached.

ON THE DOWNSTROKE, THE FEATHERS LOCK TOGETHER AND SPREAD OUT TO PROVIDE A LARGE SURFACE AREA.

THE WING'S LARGE SURFACE AREA PUSHES DOWN AGAINST THE AIR TO LIFT THE BIRD.

MAIN FLIGHT FEATHER

THE BARBS ARE ATTACHED TO THE CENTRAL STRAND, CALLED THE RACHIS.

VANE

STERNUM

FRONT-FACING EYES ALLOW OSPREYS TO SPOT A FISH IN A LAKE FROM A HEIGHT OF 100 FEET (30 METERS).

FLIGHT MUSCLES

THE BODY SHAPE IS STREAMLINED SO THE BIRD CAN EASILY CUT THE AIR.

THE BARBULES ARE LIKE HOOKS AND INTERLOCK TOGETHER.

THE UNDERSIDES OF THE TALONS ARE ROUGH TO HELP GRAB SLIPPERY FISH.

Flight feathers
Different types of feathers have different jobs. Soft down feathers close to the bird's body keep it warm. Long, flat, stiff feathers in the tail and wings are used for flight.

Each flight feather has thousands of fine strands attached to a central strand. The fine strands, called barbs, are hooked together by barbules to make a strong, flat surface.

Seeing with Sound

Animals that are active in daylight use their eyes to see. But what about creatures that move around in the dark? How do they know where to go? Marine animals that live at the dark ocean bottom and some nocturnal land animals "see" differently than other animals. Some don't use their eyes at all. These animals use sound and hearing to find where things around them are located. This method of sensing is called echolocation. Most bats, for example, use echolocation. The bats make a series of short, high-pitched sounds. The sounds waves bounce off objects in their paths. By hearing the echoes, bats are able to tell how far away an object is, if it is moving, and from what it is made.

LONG, THIN FINGER BONES SUPPORT THE WING.

A MEMBRANE OF ELASTIC SKIN STRETCHES BETWEEN THE FINGER AND ARM BONES TO FORM THE WING.

THE RIBS PROTECT THE LUNGS, HEART, LIVER, AND STOMACH.

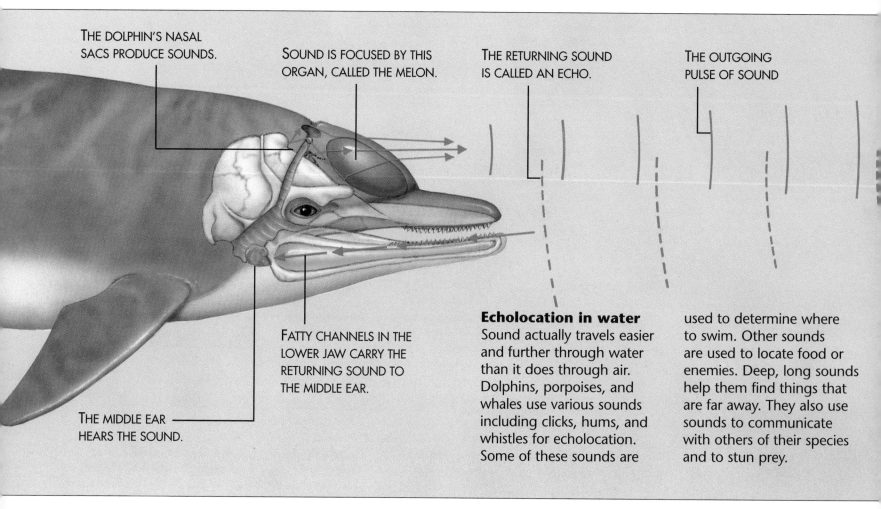

THE DOLPHIN'S NASAL SACS PRODUCE SOUNDS.

SOUND IS FOCUSED BY THIS ORGAN, CALLED THE MELON.

THE RETURNING SOUND IS CALLED AN ECHO.

THE OUTGOING PULSE OF SOUND

FATTY CHANNELS IN THE LOWER JAW CARRY THE RETURNING SOUND TO THE MIDDLE EAR.

THE MIDDLE EAR HEARS THE SOUND.

Echolocation in water
Sound actually travels easier and further through water than it does through air. Dolphins, porpoises, and whales use various sounds including clicks, hums, and whistles for echolocation. Some of these sounds are used to determine where to swim. Other sounds are used to locate food or enemies. Deep, long sounds help them find things that are far away. They also use sounds to communicate with others of their species and to stun prey.

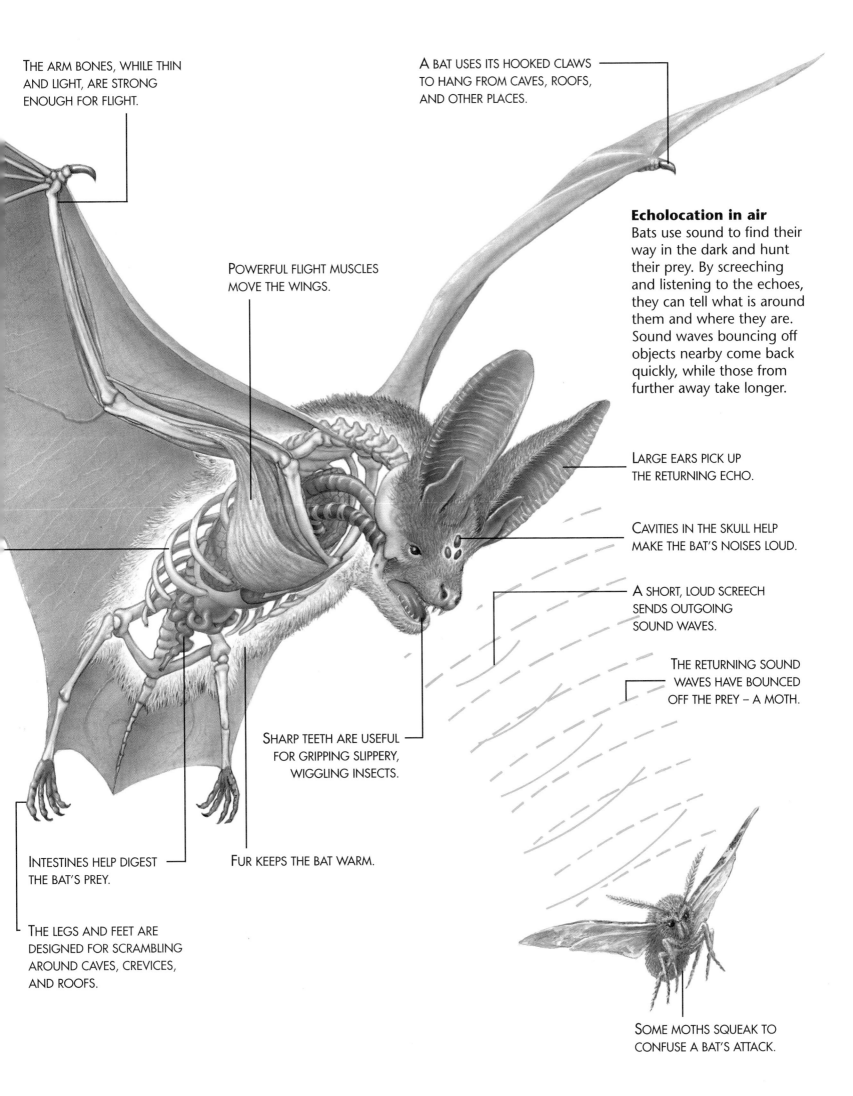

THE ARM BONES, WHILE THIN AND LIGHT, ARE STRONG ENOUGH FOR FLIGHT.

A BAT USES ITS HOOKED CLAWS TO HANG FROM CAVES, ROOFS, AND OTHER PLACES.

POWERFUL FLIGHT MUSCLES MOVE THE WINGS.

Echolocation in air
Bats use sound to find their way in the dark and hunt their prey. By screeching and listening to the echoes, they can tell what is around them and where they are. Sound waves bouncing off objects nearby come back quickly, while those from further away take longer.

LARGE EARS PICK UP THE RETURNING ECHO.

CAVITIES IN THE SKULL HELP MAKE THE BAT'S NOISES LOUD.

A SHORT, LOUD SCREECH SENDS OUTGOING SOUND WAVES.

THE RETURNING SOUND WAVES HAVE BOUNCED OFF THE PREY – A MOTH.

SHARP TEETH ARE USEFUL FOR GRIPPING SLIPPERY, WIGGLING INSECTS.

INTESTINES HELP DIGEST THE BAT'S PREY.

FUR KEEPS THE BAT WARM.

THE LEGS AND FEET ARE DESIGNED FOR SCRAMBLING AROUND CAVES, CREVICES, AND ROOFS.

SOME MOTHS SQUEAK TO CONFUSE A BAT'S ATTACK.

A Spider's Web

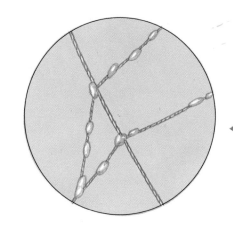

Garden spiders spin webs to catch insects that they can eat. They make their webs out of special silks that they produce in their bodies. During late summer, the large webs of adult spiders can be found among plants and bushes. Spiders wait for insects by sitting upside-down in the centers of their webs. After the insects get caught in the webs, the spiders seize and kill their victims.

Spider's silk has other uses. If a spider is frightened by a predator, it may drop to the ground on a silken safety line, which is a thread that trails from the spider's body so that it is always connected to the web. Spiders also use silk to wrap their delicate eggs and to preserve their food.

Sticky beads
The spider makes a special sticky silk to trap insects. As this silk is applied to the web's thread, the spider uses its back legs to strum the threads like guitar strings. This strumming breaks the coat into sticky beads.

SPIDERS HAVE FOUR PAIRS OF LEGS WITH EIGHT SEGMENTS ON EACH LEG.

THE STOMACH SUCKS FOOD INTO THE INTESTINE. MOUTH HAIRS TRAP ANY SOLID PARTICLES.

VENOM FROM THIS SAC IS INJECTED INTO THE SPIDER'S PREY TO TRANQUILIZE AND KILL IT.

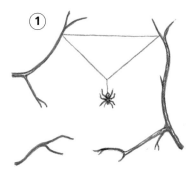

①

DANGLING ON THE LINE, THE SPIDER SPINS A Y-FORK.

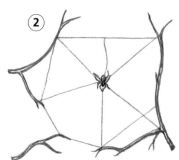

②

THE SPIDER THEN ADDS MORE SPOKES TO THE WHEEL TO MAKE A STRONG WEB.

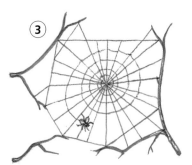

③

THE SPIDER LAYS DOWN A SUPPORTING SPIRAL BEFORE THE FINAL STICKY SPIRAL.

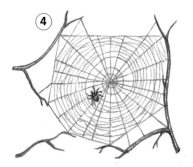

④

THE WEB IS NOW COMPLETE AND IS READY TO CATCH INSECTS.

Web spinning
To begin making its web, the spider either floats its silk across a gap so the silk catches on the other side or walks around the gap trailing the silk behind it. The silk is then pulled tight and attached. While climbing across this line, the spider puts down a stronger one. The spider spins a loose loop and creates a Y-shaped fork. More "spokes" are added, helping the spider walk across the web and wind its thread around in a spiral. The spider's long legs keep the web in an even shape as it works.

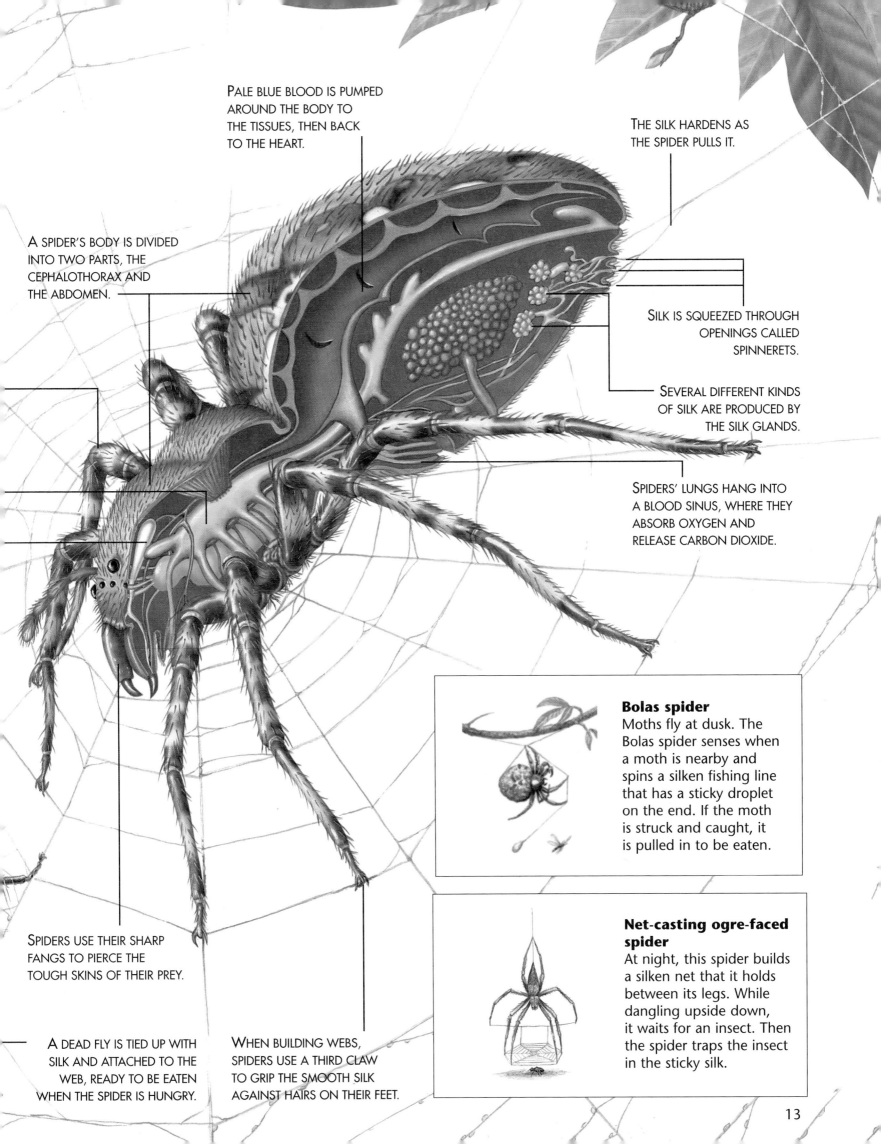

PALE BLUE BLOOD IS PUMPED AROUND THE BODY TO THE TISSUES, THEN BACK TO THE HEART.

THE SILK HARDENS AS THE SPIDER PULLS IT.

A SPIDER'S BODY IS DIVIDED INTO TWO PARTS, THE CEPHALOTHORAX AND THE ABDOMEN.

SILK IS SQUEEZED THROUGH OPENINGS CALLED SPINNERETS.

SEVERAL DIFFERENT KINDS OF SILK ARE PRODUCED BY THE SILK GLANDS.

SPIDERS' LUNGS HANG INTO A BLOOD SINUS, WHERE THEY ABSORB OXYGEN AND RELEASE CARBON DIOXIDE.

Bolas spider
Moths fly at dusk. The Bolas spider senses when a moth is nearby and spins a silken fishing line that has a sticky droplet on the end. If the moth is struck and caught, it is pulled in to be eaten.

Net-casting ogre-faced spider
At night, this spider builds a silken net that it holds between its legs. While dangling upside down, it waits for an insect. Then the spider traps the insect in the sticky silk.

SPIDERS USE THEIR SHARP FANGS TO PIERCE THE TOUGH SKINS OF THEIR PREY.

A DEAD FLY IS TIED UP WITH SILK AND ATTACHED TO THE WEB, READY TO BE EATEN WHEN THE SPIDER IS HUNGRY.

WHEN BUILDING WEBS, SPIDERS USE A THIRD CLAW TO GRIP THE SMOOTH SILK AGAINST HAIRS ON THEIR FEET.

13

Grazing Animals

Impalas are large, grazing antelopes that are found in the savannas and open woodlands of Africa. They live in herds that range from ten to several hundred individuals. Each herd is led by an older male. Younger males are guards. Impalas eat quickly to get enough food and avoid danger. If an impala is frightened by another animal, such as a lion, it makes a sneezing sound to warn the others, giving the herd enough time to bound away.

When grazing, impalas get a tight grip on grass and plants with their long tongues. Their sharp front teeth, called incisors, bite off the plants. The back teeth, called molars, have large, flattened tops for grinding and chewing. Since grass is difficult to digest, impalas chew and swallow their food a second time. This system of digestion is called rumination. Impalas move to safe places away from predators to ruminate.

A four-part stomach
Swallowed food passes into the rumen (1) where it is broken down into small balls called cud. The cud is then returned to the mouth for more chewing. After the cud is reswallowed, the food is broken down more in the the reticulum (2). Next, water is squeezed from the food in the omasum (3) and further digested in the abomasum (4). Then, it passes into the intestines.

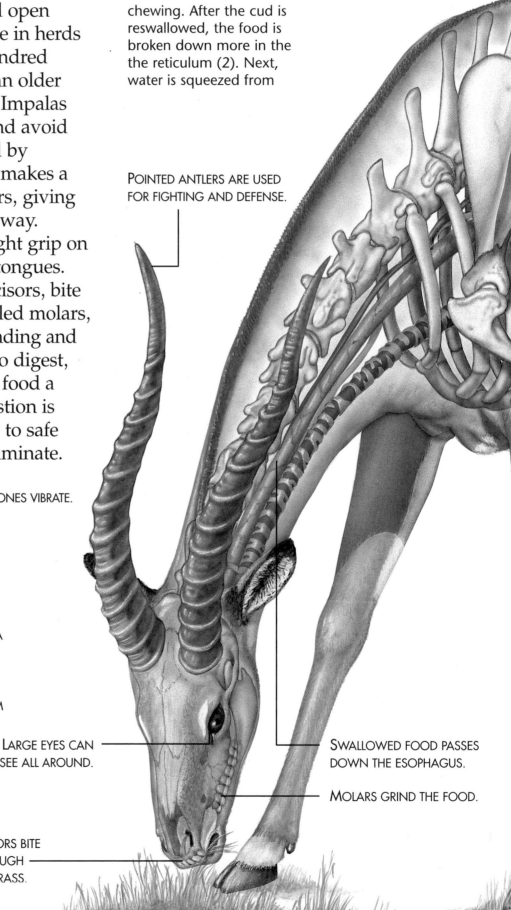

POINTED ANTLERS ARE USED FOR FIGHTING AND DEFENSE.

THREE TINY BONES VIBRATE.

THE COCHLEA

THE EARDRUM

Listening for danger
Impalas listen for danger. Sound travels into the ear and then vibrates the eardrum. Three tiny bones are moved in the process; these then move a thin membrane. This causes the liquid in the cochlea to move. The moving liquid triggers tiny hairs that send signals to the brain.

LARGE EYES CAN SEE ALL AROUND.

SHARP INCISORS BITE THROUGH TOUGH BLADES OF GRASS.

SWALLOWED FOOD PASSES DOWN THE ESOPHAGUS.

MOLARS GRIND THE FOOD.

14

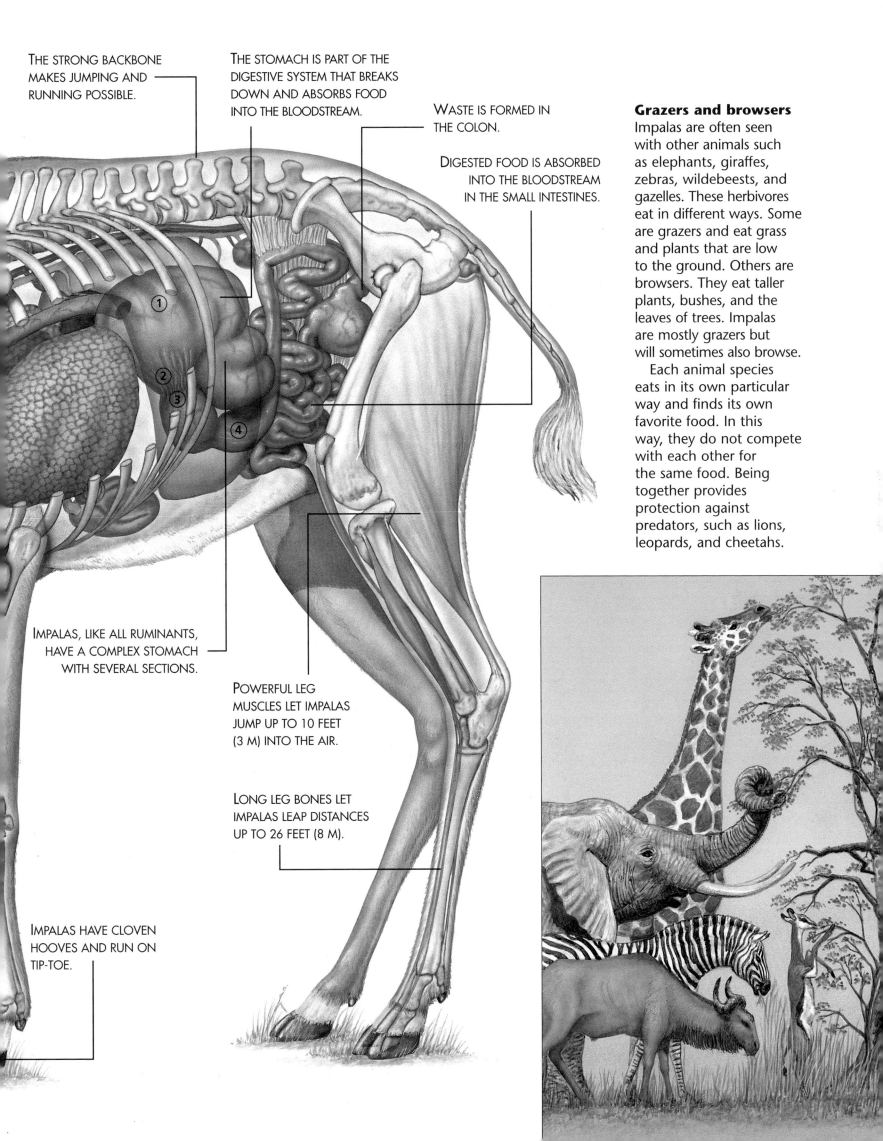

THE STRONG BACKBONE MAKES JUMPING AND RUNNING POSSIBLE.

THE STOMACH IS PART OF THE DIGESTIVE SYSTEM THAT BREAKS DOWN AND ABSORBS FOOD INTO THE BLOODSTREAM.

WASTE IS FORMED IN THE COLON.

DIGESTED FOOD IS ABSORBED INTO THE BLOODSTREAM IN THE SMALL INTESTINES.

IMPALAS, LIKE ALL RUMINANTS, HAVE A COMPLEX STOMACH WITH SEVERAL SECTIONS.

POWERFUL LEG MUSCLES LET IMPALAS JUMP UP TO 10 FEET (3 M) INTO THE AIR.

LONG LEG BONES LET IMPALAS LEAP DISTANCES UP TO 26 FEET (8 M).

IMPALAS HAVE CLOVEN HOOVES AND RUN ON TIP-TOE.

Grazers and browsers

Impalas are often seen with other animals such as elephants, giraffes, zebras, wildebeests, and gazelles. These herbivores eat in different ways. Some are grazers and eat grass and plants that are low to the ground. Others are browsers. They eat taller plants, bushes, and the leaves of trees. Impalas are mostly grazers but will sometimes also browse.

Each animal species eats in its own particular way and finds its own favorite food. In this way, they do not compete with each other for the same food. Being together provides protection against predators, such as lions, leopards, and cheetahs.

Hunters

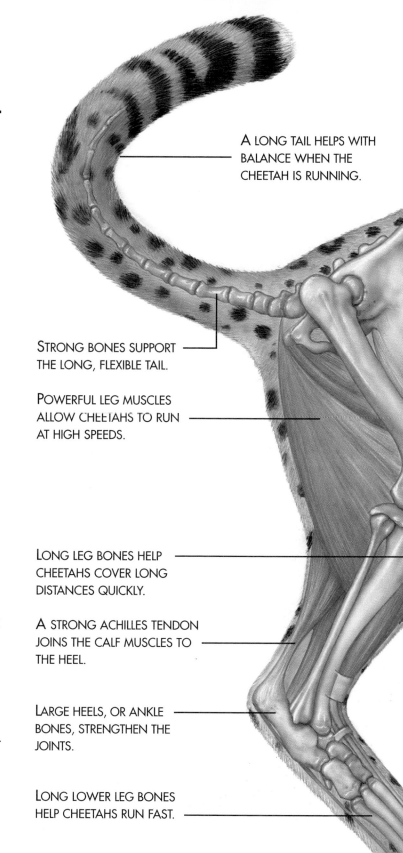

A LONG TAIL HELPS WITH BALANCE WHEN THE CHEETAH IS RUNNING.

STRONG BONES SUPPORT THE LONG, FLEXIBLE TAIL.

POWERFUL LEG MUSCLES ALLOW CHEETAHS TO RUN AT HIGH SPEEDS.

LONG LEG BONES HELP CHEETAHS COVER LONG DISTANCES QUICKLY.

A STRONG ACHILLES TENDON JOINS THE CALF MUSCLES TO THE HEEL.

LARGE HEELS, OR ANKLE BONES, STRENGTHEN THE JOINTS.

LONG LOWER LEG BONES HELP CHEETAHS RUN FAST.

nimals that hunt have special skills and body parts for catching prey. Big cats, including lions, tigers, leopards, jaguars, and cheetahs (*right*) hunt the largest animals. These cats must be clever, fast, and strong to catch prey. Their jaws are short and powerful, their skulls strong, and their teeth large and sharp to quickly tear prey apart. Long canine teeth stab their victims, and chisel-like incisors rip through tough skins. They also have razor-sharp molar teeth that help them quickly chew through flesh.

Out of all the cats, the cheetah is best known for its hunting ability. Its slim, streamlined body allows for great speed. The cheetah can reach speeds up to 70 miles (115 kilometers) per hour, making it the fastest animal on four legs.

Hunting

Cheetahs have special features that help them hunt. Their eyes are sharp, helping them see prey moving against the horizon while they hide in tall grass.

Cheetahs chase young gazelles when they are as far as 1,650 feet (500 m) away. They also prey upon adult gazelles, which are more alert than their young, but only from much closer range – about 165 feet (50 m) away.

Cheetahs cannot run at top speed for long. If they did, their bodies would overheat and they would die. To cool off, they draw in cooling air through their wide nostrils.

Once cheetahs have caught up with their prey, they need to kill and eat it quickly, as lions and hyenas could easily steal their hard-earned meals.

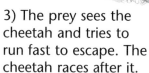

The chase

1) The cheetah stalks its victim before beginning its high-speed chase.

2) With its ears back and eyes fixed on its prey, the cheetah leaps forward and begins to build up speed.

3) The prey sees the cheetah and tries to run fast to escape. The cheetah races after it.

The cheetah matches the prey's speed and path before trying to knock it over.

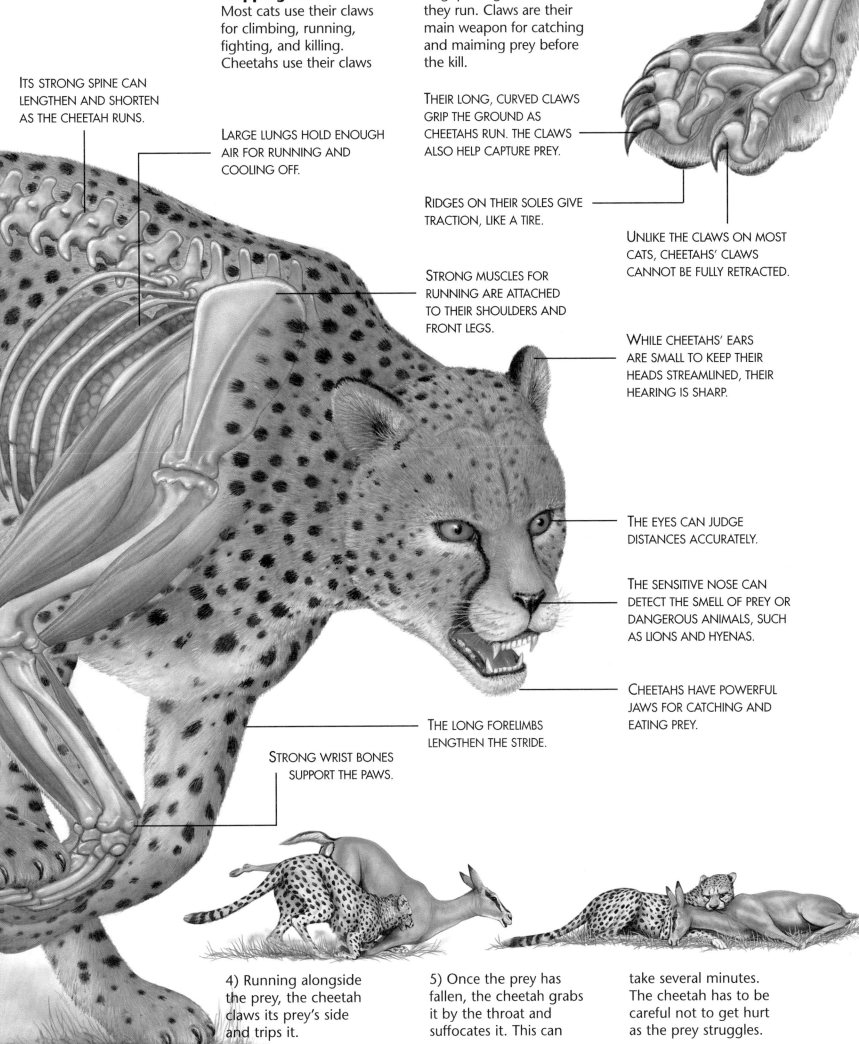

Gripping claws
Most cats use their claws for climbing, running, fighting, and killing. Cheetahs use their claws to grip the ground while they run. Claws are their main weapon for catching and maiming prey before the kill.

ITS STRONG SPINE CAN LENGTHEN AND SHORTEN AS THE CHEETAH RUNS.

LARGE LUNGS HOLD ENOUGH AIR FOR RUNNING AND COOLING OFF.

THEIR LONG, CURVED CLAWS GRIP THE GROUND AS CHEETAHS RUN. THE CLAWS ALSO HELP CAPTURE PREY.

RIDGES ON THEIR SOLES GIVE TRACTION, LIKE A TIRE.

UNLIKE THE CLAWS ON MOST CATS, CHEETAHS' CLAWS CANNOT BE FULLY RETRACTED.

STRONG MUSCLES FOR RUNNING ARE ATTACHED TO THEIR SHOULDERS AND FRONT LEGS.

WHILE CHEETAHS' EARS ARE SMALL TO KEEP THEIR HEADS STREAMLINED, THEIR HEARING IS SHARP.

THE EYES CAN JUDGE DISTANCES ACCURATELY.

THE SENSITIVE NOSE CAN DETECT THE SMELL OF PREY OR DANGEROUS ANIMALS, SUCH AS LIONS AND HYENAS.

CHEETAHS HAVE POWERFUL JAWS FOR CATCHING AND EATING PREY.

THE LONG FORELIMBS LENGTHEN THE STRIDE.

STRONG WRIST BONES SUPPORT THE PAWS.

4) Running alongside the prey, the cheetah claws its prey's side and trips it.

5) Once the prey has fallen, the cheetah grabs it by the throat and suffocates it. This can take several minutes. The cheetah has to be careful not to get hurt as the prey struggles.

Snakes

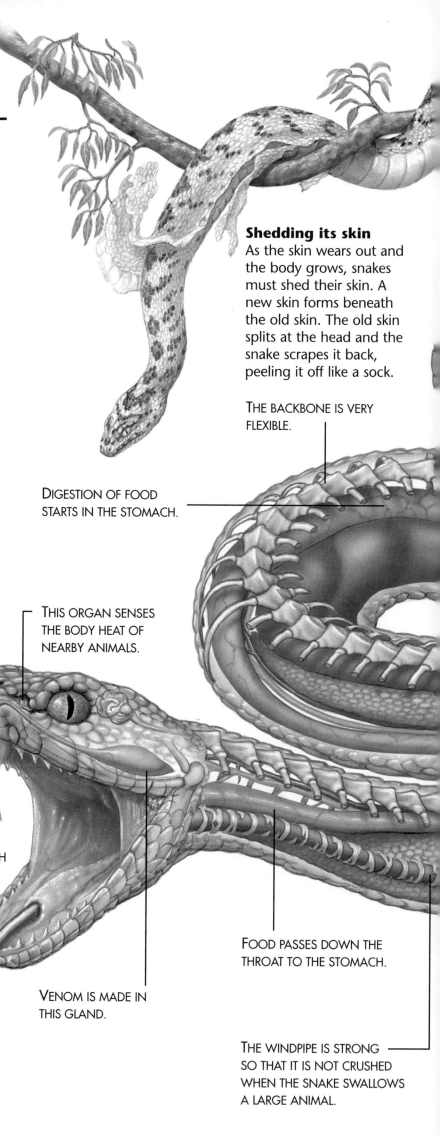

The green bamboo tree viper lives in Southeast Asia and can grow up to 3 feet (1 m) long. Green bamboo tree vipers have strong tails and rough scales to grasp twigs and leaves, allowing them to climb and live in trees. They eat small mammals, birds, lizards, and frogs. Before they are born, baby vipers hatch out of their eggs while they are still inside their mother's body. About a dozen baby vipers are born at one time.

Many snakes are poisonous. They inject their prey with venom as they bite them. Venom can kill prey so that it is ready to eat. Some snakes, however, do not use venom. These snakes either grab and eat their prey quickly or slowly coil their bodies around it and squeeze it until it suffocates.

Shedding its skin
As the skin wears out and the body grows, snakes must shed their skin. A new skin forms beneath the old skin. The old skin splits at the head and the snake scrapes it back, peeling it off like a sock.

THE BACKBONE IS VERY FLEXIBLE.

DIGESTION OF FOOD STARTS IN THE STOMACH.

THIS ORGAN SENSES THE BODY HEAT OF NEARBY ANIMALS.

<u>CLOSED MOUTH</u>

THE FANGS ARE TUCKED INSIDE.

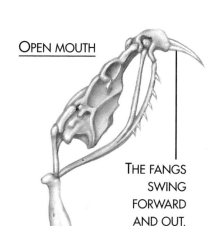

<u>OPEN MOUTH</u>

THE FANGS SWING FORWARD AND OUT.

VENOM FROM THE POISON GLANDS IS INJECTED THROUGH THE SYRINGELIKE FANGS.

THE FORKED TONGUE CAN "TASTE" ANY SMELLS IN THE AIR.

VENOM IS MADE IN THIS GLAND.

FOOD PASSES DOWN THE THROAT TO THE STOMACH.

THE WINDPIPE IS STRONG SO THAT IT IS NOT CRUSHED WHEN THE SNAKE SWALLOWS A LARGE ANIMAL.

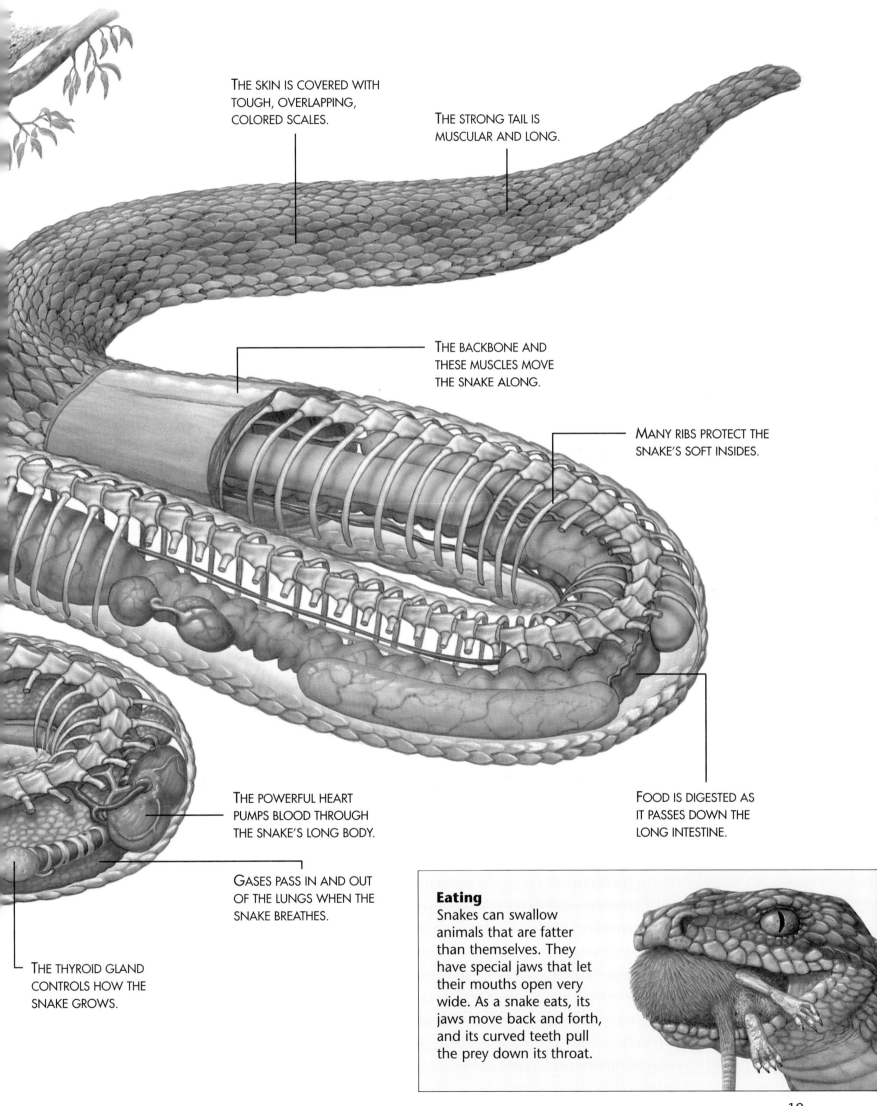

THE SKIN IS COVERED WITH TOUGH, OVERLAPPING, COLORED SCALES.

THE STRONG TAIL IS MUSCULAR AND LONG.

THE BACKBONE AND THESE MUSCLES MOVE THE SNAKE ALONG.

MANY RIBS PROTECT THE SNAKE'S SOFT INSIDES.

THE POWERFUL HEART PUMPS BLOOD THROUGH THE SNAKE'S LONG BODY.

FOOD IS DIGESTED AS IT PASSES DOWN THE LONG INTESTINE.

GASES PASS IN AND OUT OF THE LUNGS WHEN THE SNAKE BREATHES.

THE THYROID GLAND CONTROLS HOW THE SNAKE GROWS.

Eating
Snakes can swallow animals that are fatter than themselves. They have special jaws that let their mouths open very wide. As a snake eats, its jaws move back and forth, and its curved teeth pull the prey down its throat.

Sea Mammals

Whales, seals, and sea lions are all marine mammals. As mammals, they are warm-blooded, breathe air through lungs, and give birth to live young that nurse, or drink, their milk. Seals and sea lions do not only live in the sea. They come on shore to rest and raise their young. Whales, however, spend their whole lives in the sea. They never go on land except by accident, when they become beached, or stranded.

Whales are perfectly evolved for ocean life. They are smooth and streamlined, and have powerful tails, making them excellent swimmers. Even though they often swim in deep waters where there is no light, they know where they are by using sound. This system of "seeing" is called echolocation (*see pages 10-11*).

Blowhole
Whales' nostrils are on top of their heads. They close up when the whales travel under water. As the whales surface, air in their lungs expands and is forced out through the blowhole.

AS THE WHALE SURFACES, AIR IN THE LUNGS EXPANDS AND IS FORCED OUT.

THE BLOWHOLE IS CLOSED AS THE WHALE SWIMS UNDERWATER.

CROSS SECTIONS OF A WHALE'S BLOWHOLE.

A HUMPBACK WHALE CAN WEIGH UP TO 40 TONS.

WORMS AND OTHER CREATURES LIVE IN THE HORNY KNOBS OF WHALES' SKIN.

THE BALEEN ARE ATTACHED TO THE UPPER JAW.

Baleen
Two hard brushlike sheets, called baleen, hang down from the upper jaw inside some whales' mouths. Each of the sheets is covered with hundreds of fine bristles. As their mouths open, water floods in, often carrying with it tiny shrimplike creatures called krill. When their mouths close, the water is forced out through the bristles, trapping the krill inside.

THE TONGUE SQUEEZES WATER FROM THE MOUTH, SCRAPES KRILL FROM THE BALEEN, AND PUSHES IT DOWN THE THROAT.

THE JAWS OPEN VERY WIDE WHEN THE WHALE EATS.

PLEATS, OR FOLDS IN THE SKIN, UNFOLD AS THE MOUTH FILLS WITH WATER.

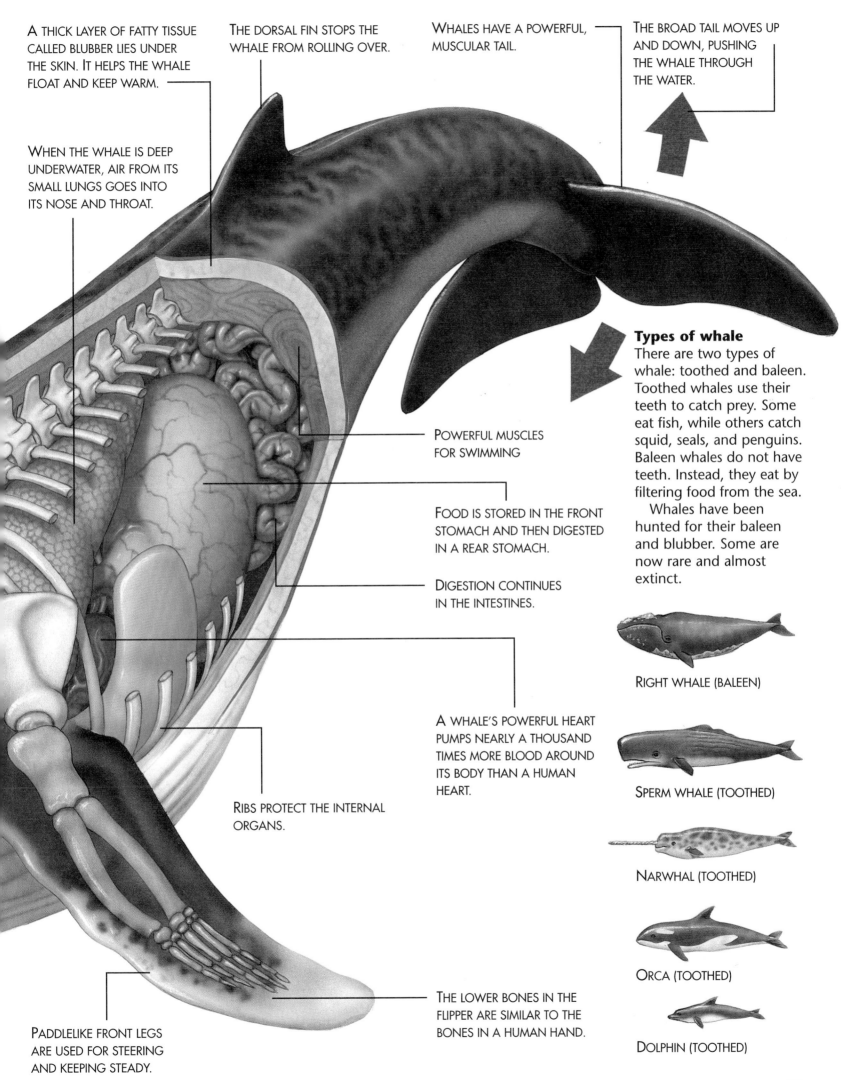

A THICK LAYER OF FATTY TISSUE CALLED BLUBBER LIES UNDER THE SKIN. IT HELPS THE WHALE FLOAT AND KEEP WARM.

WHEN THE WHALE IS DEEP UNDERWATER, AIR FROM ITS SMALL LUNGS GOES INTO ITS NOSE AND THROAT.

THE DORSAL FIN STOPS THE WHALE FROM ROLLING OVER.

WHALES HAVE A POWERFUL, MUSCULAR TAIL.

THE BROAD TAIL MOVES UP AND DOWN, PUSHING THE WHALE THROUGH THE WATER.

POWERFUL MUSCLES FOR SWIMMING

FOOD IS STORED IN THE FRONT STOMACH AND THEN DIGESTED IN A REAR STOMACH.

DIGESTION CONTINUES IN THE INTESTINES.

A WHALE'S POWERFUL HEART PUMPS NEARLY A THOUSAND TIMES MORE BLOOD AROUND ITS BODY THAN A HUMAN HEART.

RIBS PROTECT THE INTERNAL ORGANS.

PADDLELIKE FRONT LEGS ARE USED FOR STEERING AND KEEPING STEADY.

THE LOWER BONES IN THE FLIPPER ARE SIMILAR TO THE BONES IN A HUMAN HAND.

Types of whale

There are two types of whale: toothed and baleen. Toothed whales use their teeth to catch prey. Some eat fish, while others catch squid, seals, and penguins. Baleen whales do not have teeth. Instead, they eat by filtering food from the sea.

Whales have been hunted for their baleen and blubber. Some are now rare and almost extinct.

RIGHT WHALE (BALEEN)

SPERM WHALE (TOOTHED)

NARWHAL (TOOTHED)

ORCA (TOOTHED)

DOLPHIN (TOOTHED)

Self-defense

Animals must defend themselves against attack, and they do so in many different ways. For example, some animals fight to defend themselves. These animals might be big and fierce, armed with sharp teeth, poison fangs, or strong, sharp claws. Gentle animals, such as antelope, can also be violent, using their antlers to fight enemies. Some animals change the color of their bodies to disguise themselves. This is called camouflage. They change to match their surroundings, making themselves invisible to predators. They may look like leaves or rocks. Others change into a shape that is hard to attack. Yet other creatures have special defenses. Porcupines shoot quills, camels spit, and bees sting.

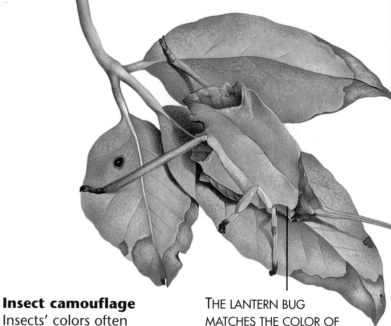

Insect camouflage
Insects' colors often match their surroundings. They hide among the leaves and stems of plants where they live. As they eat, the insects move slowly to avoid drawing too much attention to themselves.

THE LANTERN BUG MATCHES THE COLOR OF THE LEAVES AROUND IT.

A prickly ball
Hedgehogs are bold animals that are noisy at night, hunting for worms, insects, snails, and even small snakes. They are able to be bold because they are protected from most predators by the stiff quills on their backs and sides. The quills are actually hollow, sharp hairs. When frightened, hedgehogs roll up into tight, prickly balls as their muscles contract and shorten.

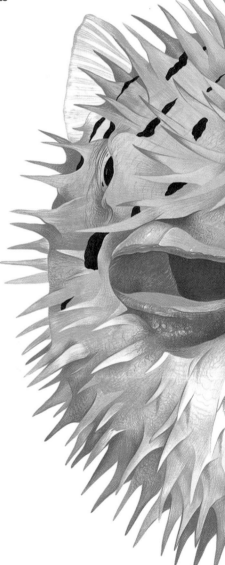

THE HEDGEHOG ROLLS INTO A BALL IF IT IS FRIGHTENED.

THE QUILLS LIE FLAT UNLESS THERE IS DANGER.

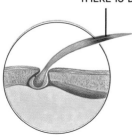

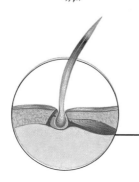

AS THE SPINE MUSCLES CONTRACT, THE QUILLS ARE RAISED.

WHEN THE BODY IS DEFLATED, THE SPINES LIE FLAT.

Colorful chameleons

Chameleons are gentle, slow-moving lizards that often change color to match their surroundings. They also change color depending on their mood. When a chameleon becomes angry, a brown substance in its skin, called melanin, is pushed to the surface. This process darkens the animal's color. Other colors are produced by special red, yellow, blue, and white cells in its skin. When a chameleon is calm, its skin is green. Green is produced when the yellow skin cells enlarge over the blue cells. The chameleon changes color quickly, and the change is controlled by the brain and chemicals in its blood.

THE CHAMELEON'S MUSCULAR, STICKY-TIPPED TONGUE DARTS OUT OF ITS MOUTH TO CATCH AN INSECT.

A CHAMELEON'S EYES STICK OUT AND GIVE IT VISION ALL AROUND.

THE SKIN IS MADE UP OF MILLIONS OF CELLS.

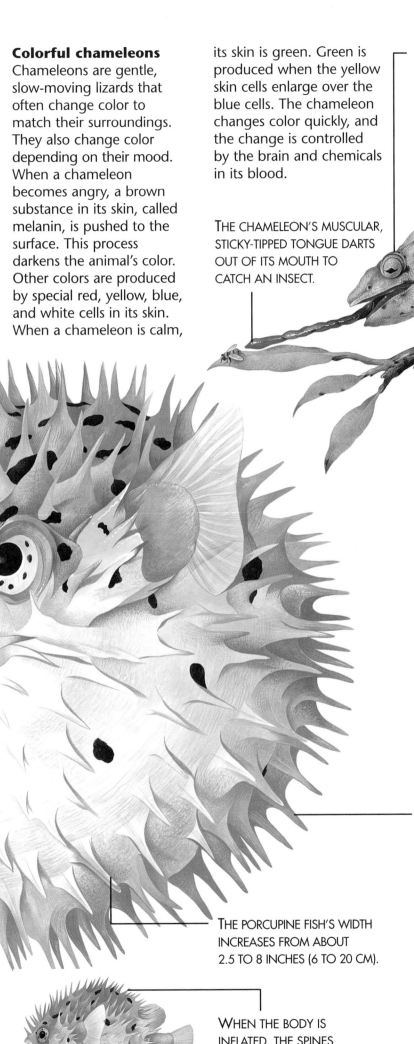

COLORED SKIN CELLS EXPAND AND SHRINK TO MAKE DIFFERENT COLORS.

FINGERS AND TOES PROVIDE A FIRM GRIP.

Porcupine fish

Porcupine fish do not swim fast, but they have evolved to survive well. An armor of spines protects them. When threatened, they inflate their bodies like a balloon by swallowing water or air. Once inflated, the porcupine fish float, often upside down. As floating balls of spines, they are nearly impossible for predators to bite, let alone swallow!

Tortoise shell

Tortoises and their cousins, turtles and terrapins, live inside a tough, protective shell. When they are in danger, they can hide their legs, head, and tail inside their shells. The shell is made of bony plates that fit together like a puzzle. A tough, horny layer covers and protects the whole shell. The tortoise's body is attached to the shell along the backbone and at the hips and shoulders.

THE NORMALLY SMALL PORCUPINE FISH GROWS INTO A PRICKLY BALL OF SPINES.

THE TORTOISE'S LEGS, TAIL, AND HEAD ARE TUCKED INSIDE THE SHELL.

THE PORCUPINE FISH'S WIDTH INCREASES FROM ABOUT 2.5 TO 8 INCHES (6 TO 20 CM).

WHEN THE BODY IS INFLATED, THE SPINES STICK OUT.

Inside Shells

Some animals live inside shells. Many of these animals belong to the mollusk family, which includes snails, clams, and mussels. Octopi and squid are also mollusks, but they do not live in shells. Mollusks live in water — such as rivers, lakes, ponds, and seas — and also on land. Their bodies are made up of four parts: the head, the muscular foot, the hump, and the mantle. The head is made up of eyes, tentacles, and a mouth. The hump holds the internal organs and is located above the muscular foot. The mantle is a thin sheet of tissue that grows over the hump and produces the shell, which is a tough, chalky substance. Between the body tissues and the mantle are the gills and openings from the intestine, reproductive organs, and kidneys.

Spiral shell

Scientists know about over 75,000 different kinds of snails. Each snail lives in its own type of shell. The shell has an opening, called the aperture, and is usually twisted into a spiral. Each spiral twist is called a whorl.

Shells are colored either for camouflage or to warn predators of their poison. The largest snail, the trumpet conch, can reach over 177 inches (450 cm) long, while the smallest, the pupa, is less than .16 inch (4 millimeters) long.

Snail

Snails glide on a large foot. The foot does not simply help them get from place to place; it is also joined with the head and contains many of the snail's organs, including the brain, eyes, tentacles, and mouth. This is why snails are called gastropods, which means "stomach-foot." Their long, coiled intestines are tucked inside their shells with their kidneys and reproductive organs. Snails mostly eat plant material, but some eat other snails by drilling holes into their shells.

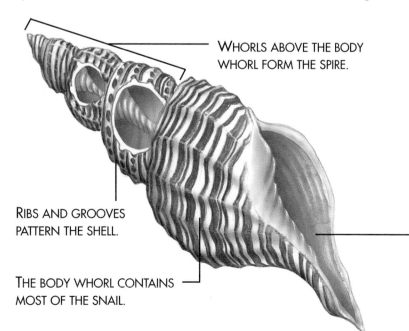

WHORLS ABOVE THE BODY WHORL FORM THE SPIRE.

RIBS AND GROOVES PATTERN THE SHELL.

THE BODY WHORL CONTAINS MOST OF THE SNAIL.

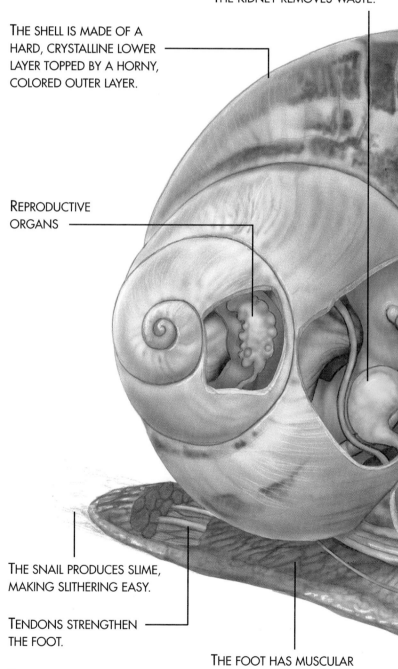

THE KIDNEY REMOVES WASTE.

THE SHELL IS MADE OF A HARD, CRYSTALLINE LOWER LAYER TOPPED BY A HORNY, COLORED OUTER LAYER.

REPRODUCTIVE ORGANS

THE SNAIL PRODUCES SLIME, MAKING SLITHERING EASY.

TENDONS STRENGTHEN THE FOOT.

THE BODY AND FOOT EXTEND THROUGH THE APERTURE.

THE FOOT HAS MUSCULAR RIPPLES TO HELP GUIDE THE SNAIL.

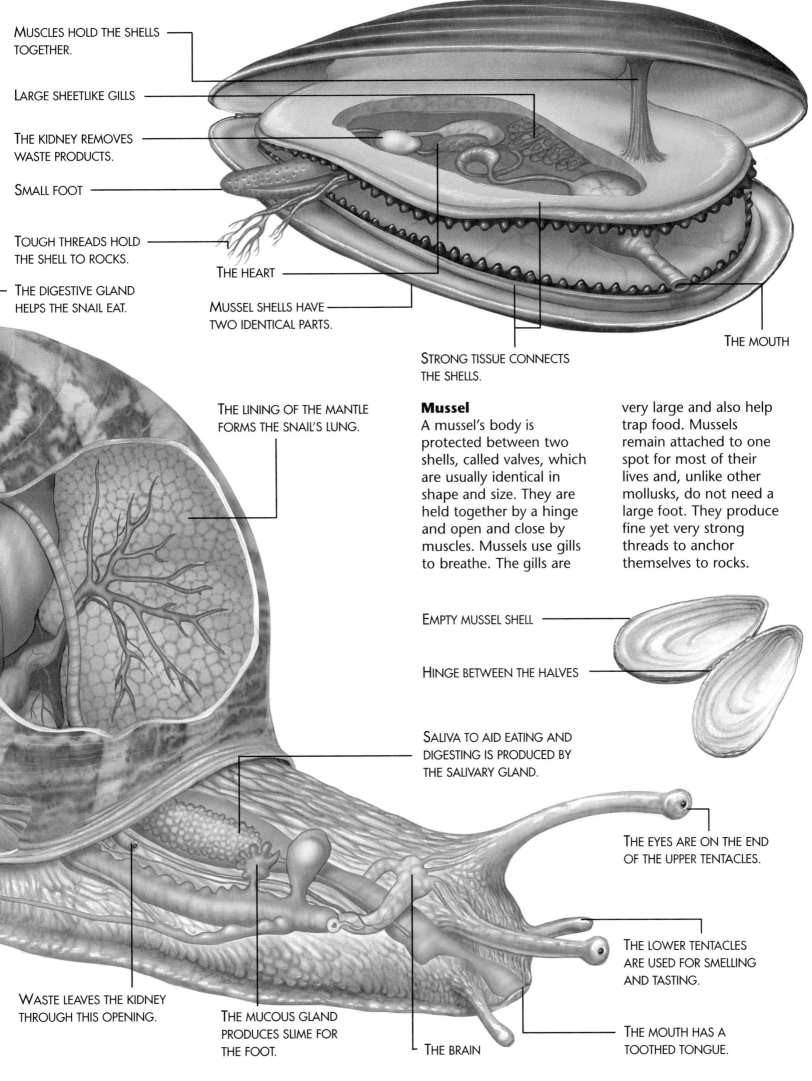

MUSCLES HOLD THE SHELLS TOGETHER.

LARGE SHEETLIKE GILLS

THE KIDNEY REMOVES WASTE PRODUCTS.

SMALL FOOT

TOUGH THREADS HOLD THE SHELL TO ROCKS.

THE DIGESTIVE GLAND HELPS THE SNAIL EAT.

THE HEART

MUSSEL SHELLS HAVE TWO IDENTICAL PARTS.

STRONG TISSUE CONNECTS THE SHELLS.

THE MOUTH

THE LINING OF THE MANTLE FORMS THE SNAIL'S LUNG.

Mussel

A mussel's body is protected between two shells, called valves, which are usually identical in shape and size. They are held together by a hinge and open and close by muscles. Mussels use gills to breathe. The gills are very large and also help trap food. Mussels remain attached to one spot for most of their lives and, unlike other mollusks, do not need a large foot. They produce fine yet very strong threads to anchor themselves to rocks.

EMPTY MUSSEL SHELL

HINGE BETWEEN THE HALVES

SALIVA TO AID EATING AND DIGESTING IS PRODUCED BY THE SALIVARY GLAND.

THE EYES ARE ON THE END OF THE UPPER TENTACLES.

THE LOWER TENTACLES ARE USED FOR SMELLING AND TASTING.

WASTE LEAVES THE KIDNEY THROUGH THIS OPENING.

THE MUCOUS GLAND PRODUCES SLIME FOR THE FOOT.

THE BRAIN

THE MOUTH HAS A TOOTHED TONGUE.

25

Spineless Life

Some animals do not have backbones. These types of animals are called invertebrates. This group includes corals, worms, insects, and snails. Their bodies are supported by firm tissue, bags of gas or liquid, or hard outer skeletons. Animals without hard skeletons can make a soft, easy meal to a predator, so some hide in tubes or burrows. Others are able to defend themselves with spines and stings.

The Portuguese man-of-war is a soft-bodied invertebrate. It is unusual because it is made up of polyps. There are three kinds of polyps. Some take in food, some reproduce, and some sting prey. The Portuguese man-of-war drifts along on the warm seas, kept afloat by a bladder full of gas, which also acts as a sail. Its tentacles hang down below its body, trapping fish that it then stings and eats.

Deadly weapons

The tentacles on a man-of-war carry special cells called nematocytes that contain deadly weapons. When touched, they fire barbs with poison-filled threads. The barbs pierce the prey's skin, injecting it with poison. Once fired, the barbs are replaced by new ones.

EACH POISONOUS CELL HAS A TRIGGER.

CELLS THAT HAVE BEEN FIRED ARE REPLACED.

SHARP BARBS WITH POISON-FILLED THREADS STICK TO THE MAN-OF-WAR'S PREY.

THE GAS-FILLED BLADDER ACTS AS A SAIL.

A WEB OF NERVE CELLS CARRIES INFORMATION TO THE DIFFERENT PARTS OF THE MAN-OF-WAR.

POLYPS HAVE DIFFERENT FUNCTIONS, INCLUDING EATING, STINGING, AND REPRODUCING.

THE EATING POLYPS CONTRACT, PULLING PREY UP TO BE DIGESTED IN THE STOMACH.

DOZENS OF TENTACLES, HANGING DOWN UP TO 165 FEET (50 M), ARE USED TO SNARE PASSING PREY.

THE PREY IS STUNNED BY THE POISONOUS STINGS AND PULLED UP BY THE TENTACLES.

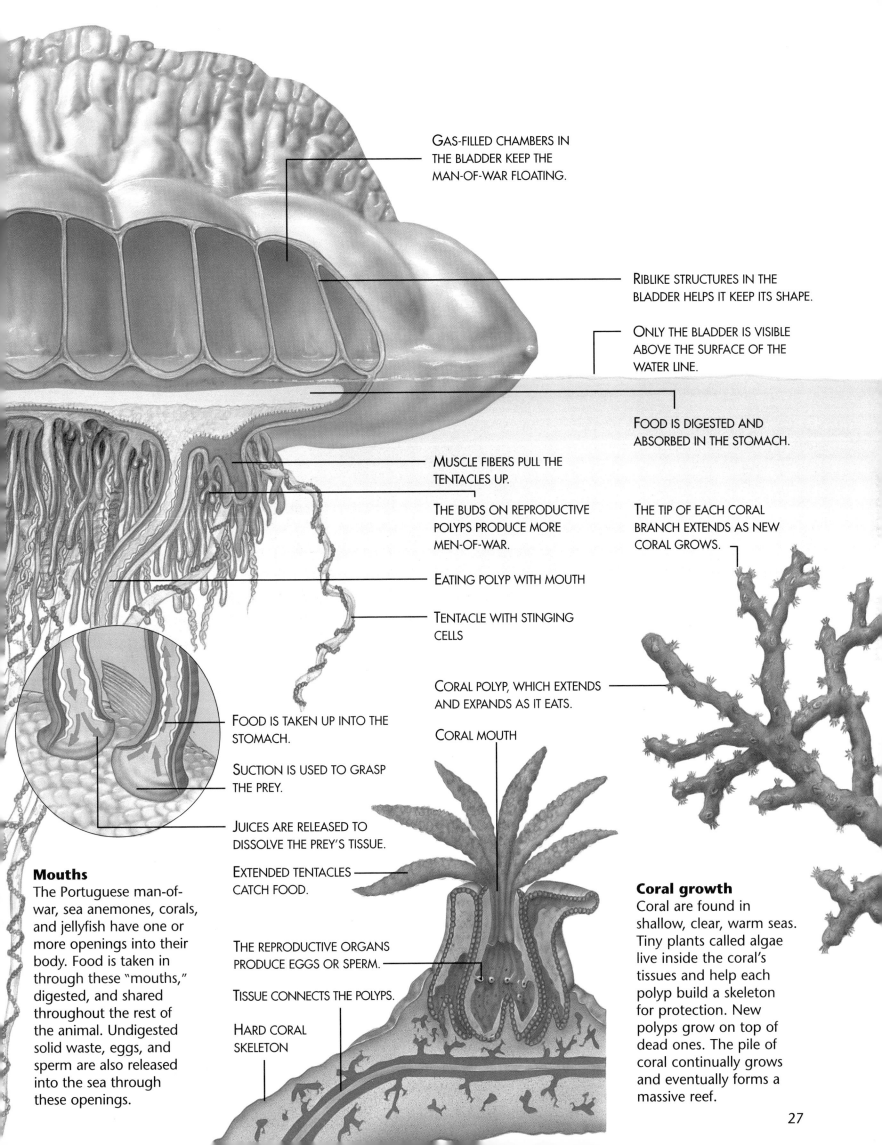

GAS-FILLED CHAMBERS IN THE BLADDER KEEP THE MAN-OF-WAR FLOATING.

RIBLIKE STRUCTURES IN THE BLADDER HELPS IT KEEP ITS SHAPE.

ONLY THE BLADDER IS VISIBLE ABOVE THE SURFACE OF THE WATER LINE.

FOOD IS DIGESTED AND ABSORBED IN THE STOMACH.

MUSCLE FIBERS PULL THE TENTACLES UP.

THE BUDS ON REPRODUCTIVE POLYPS PRODUCE MORE MEN-OF-WAR.

THE TIP OF EACH CORAL BRANCH EXTENDS AS NEW CORAL GROWS.

EATING POLYP WITH MOUTH

TENTACLE WITH STINGING CELLS

CORAL POLYP, WHICH EXTENDS AND EXPANDS AS IT EATS.

CORAL MOUTH

FOOD IS TAKEN UP INTO THE STOMACH.

SUCTION IS USED TO GRASP THE PREY.

JUICES ARE RELEASED TO DISSOLVE THE PREY'S TISSUE.

EXTENDED TENTACLES CATCH FOOD.

Mouths

The Portuguese man-of-war, sea anemones, corals, and jellyfish have one or more openings into their body. Food is taken in through these "mouths," digested, and shared throughout the rest of the animal. Undigested solid waste, eggs, and sperm are also released into the sea through these openings.

THE REPRODUCTIVE ORGANS PRODUCE EGGS OR SPERM.

TISSUE CONNECTS THE POLYPS.

HARD CORAL SKELETON

Coral growth

Coral are found in shallow, clear, warm seas. Tiny plants called algae live inside the coral's tissues and help each polyp build a skeleton for protection. New polyps grow on top of dead ones. The pile of coral continually grows and eventually forms a massive reef.

27

Insect Life

There are more individual insects and more different types of insects than any other animal. Insects live almost everywhere, from the dark, damp forest floor to the dry, hot desert. Their bodies are covered by a protective armor called a cuticle. Insect body parts can be soft and flexible or very hard. For example, the jaw of a cockroach is hard enough to cut through a lead pipe! Cuticles are also waterproof — a main reason why insect life thrives worldwide.

An insect's body is divided into three parts: the head, the thorax, and the abdomen. The head holds the eyes, antennae, mouth, and brain. The thorax supports the wings and three pairs of legs and is the powerhouse for the insect's movement. The abdomen holds the intestines and other internal organs.

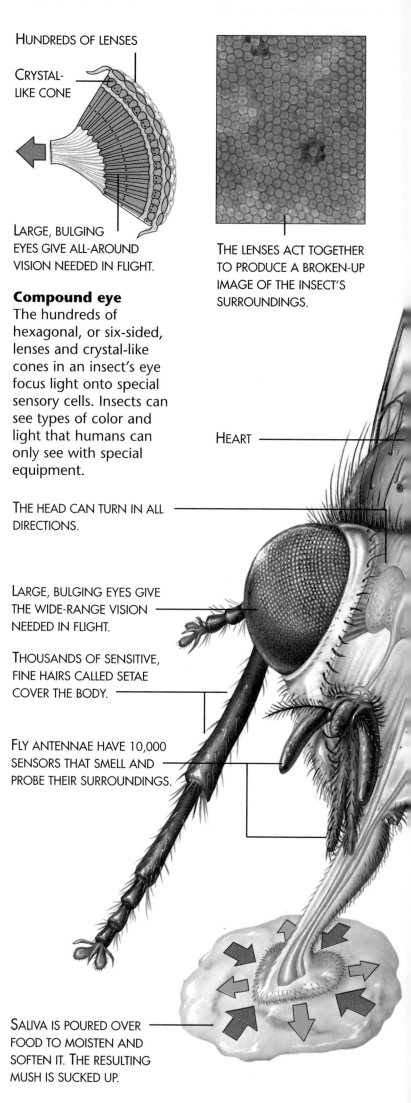

HUNDREDS OF LENSES

CRYSTAL-LIKE CONE

LARGE, BULGING EYES GIVE ALL-AROUND VISION NEEDED IN FLIGHT.

THE LENSES ACT TOGETHER TO PRODUCE A BROKEN-UP IMAGE OF THE INSECT'S SURROUNDINGS.

Compound eye
The hundreds of hexagonal, or six-sided, lenses and crystal-like cones in an insect's eye focus light onto special sensory cells. Insects can see types of color and light that humans can only see with special equipment.

THE HEAD CAN TURN IN ALL DIRECTIONS.

HEART

LARGE, BULGING EYES GIVE THE WIDE-RANGE VISION NEEDED IN FLIGHT.

THOUSANDS OF SENSITIVE, FINE HAIRS CALLED SETAE COVER THE BODY.

FLY ANTENNAE HAVE 10,000 SENSORS THAT SMELL AND PROBE THEIR SURROUNDINGS.

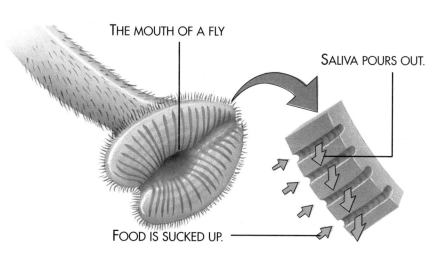

THE MOUTH OF A FLY

SALIVA POURS OUT.

FOOD IS SUCKED UP.

Tools for eating
Insects have three sets of "jaws," or mouth parts. These parts can vary drastically between different species. Some insect mouths chew. Others bite or cut. Still other insects stab, pierce, rasp, pinch, drill, inject, or lick.

Flies eat almost any liquid or semi-liquid food, from rotting filth to nectar. Saliva pours down from the fly's salivary glands onto the food. The saliva mixes with the food and softens it. The fly then uses its delicate tubes to suck the meal up directly into its stomach.

SALIVA IS POURED OVER FOOD TO MOISTEN AND SOFTEN IT. THE RESULTING MUSH IS SUCKED UP.

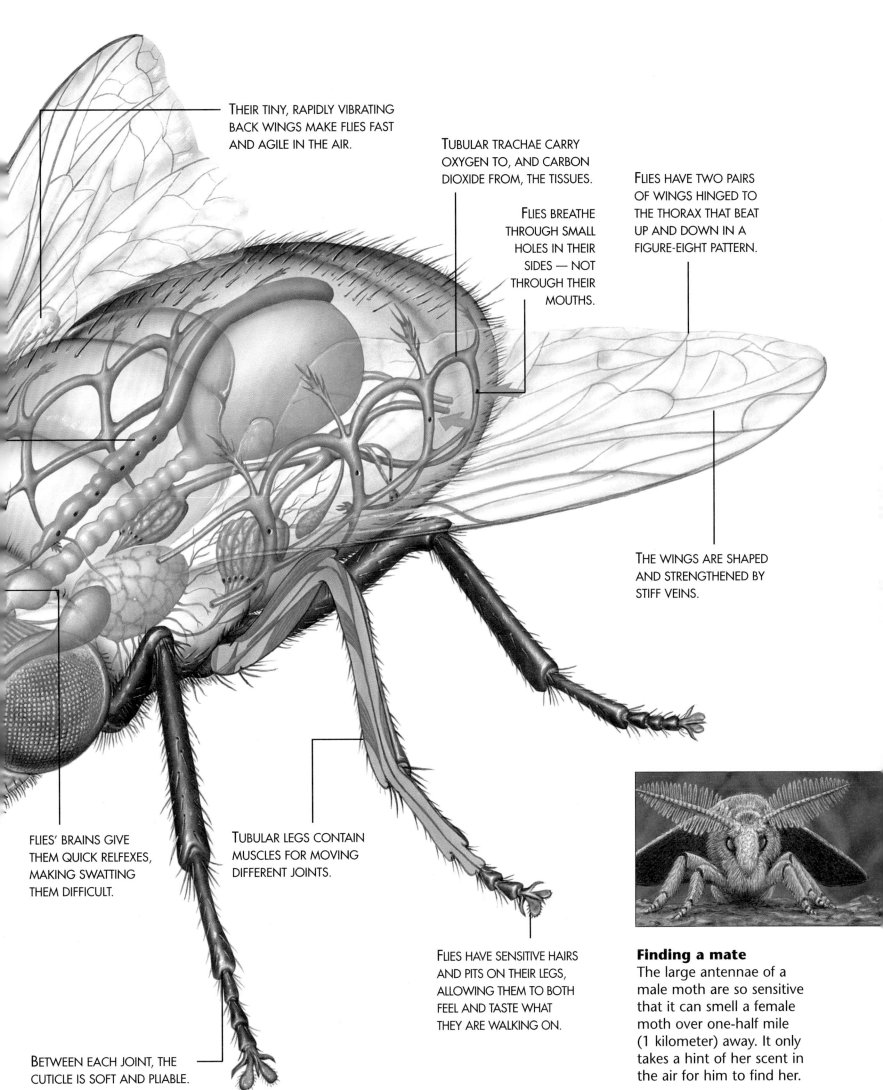

THEIR TINY, RAPIDLY VIBRATING BACK WINGS MAKE FLIES FAST AND AGILE IN THE AIR.

TUBULAR TRACHAE CARRY OXYGEN TO, AND CARBON DIOXIDE FROM, THE TISSUES.

FLIES BREATHE THROUGH SMALL HOLES IN THEIR SIDES — NOT THROUGH THEIR MOUTHS.

FLIES HAVE TWO PAIRS OF WINGS HINGED TO THE THORAX THAT BEAT UP AND DOWN IN A FIGURE-EIGHT PATTERN.

THE WINGS ARE SHAPED AND STRENGTHENED BY STIFF VEINS.

FLIES' BRAINS GIVE THEM QUICK RELFEXES, MAKING SWATTING THEM DIFFICULT.

TUBULAR LEGS CONTAIN MUSCLES FOR MOVING DIFFERENT JOINTS.

BETWEEN EACH JOINT, THE CUTICLE IS SOFT AND PLIABLE.

FLIES HAVE SENSITIVE HAIRS AND PITS ON THEIR LEGS, ALLOWING THEM TO BOTH FEEL AND TASTE WHAT THEY ARE WALKING ON.

Finding a mate
The large antennae of a male moth are so sensitive that it can smell a female moth over one-half mile (1 kilometer) away. It only takes a hint of her scent in the air for him to find her.

Changing Shape

Monarch butterflies live in North America. Like all butterflies, they begin their lives as caterpillars. While they are caterpillars, monarchs eat the leaves of milkweed plants. Although milkweed is poisonous to other animals, it is healthy for monarch caterpillars. In fact, they also use it for self-defense. They store it in their bodies, and it makes them taste so bad that predators leave them alone, even after they have become butterflies.

Caterpillars become butterflies through a process called metamorphosis. During metamorphosis, caterpillars change shape from their original form into butterfly form. Like all butterflies, monarch butterflies drink nectar from flowers. Nectar provides butterflies with the energy that they need to fly. They fly to new places to find plants on which to lay their eggs. They also fly to escape predators or to find a mate.

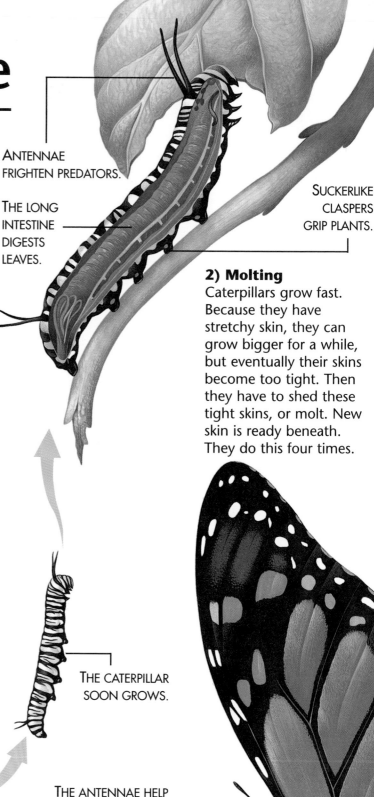

ANTENNAE FRIGHTEN PREDATORS.

THE LONG INTESTINE DIGESTS LEAVES.

SUCKERLIKE CLASPERS GRIP PLANTS.

2) Molting
Caterpillars grow fast. Because they have stretchy skin, they can grow bigger for a while, but eventually their skins become too tight. Then they have to shed these tight skins, or molt. New skin is ready beneath. They do this four times.

THE CATERPILLAR SOON GROWS.

THE ANTENNAE HELP FIND FOOD AND A MATE.

THE BRAIN

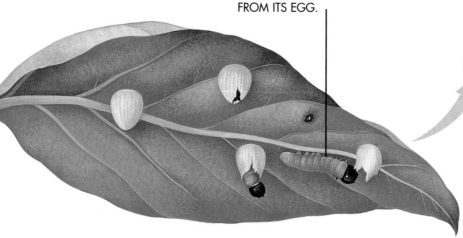

A BABY CATERPILLAR CLIMBING FROM ITS EGG.

ITS COMPOUND EYES ARE LIKE A FLY'S EYES (*see page 28*).

ITS LONG, COILED TONGUE EXTRACTS NECTAR.

1) From egg to caterpillar
Female monarch butterflies lay small groups of eggs on leaves. Some other butterflies lay their eggs singly, instead of in groups. Although the eggs are tiny, they are very tough. The eggs protect the baby caterpillars growing inside them from rain, sun, and parasites. In order to hatch from the eggs, the baby caterpillars chew their way out using their tiny jaws. After they hatch, the little caterpillars eat the egg shells before they crawl away to milkweed.

THE UPPER BODY, CALLED THE THORAX, HOLDS THE MUSCLES THAT MOVE THE WINGS.

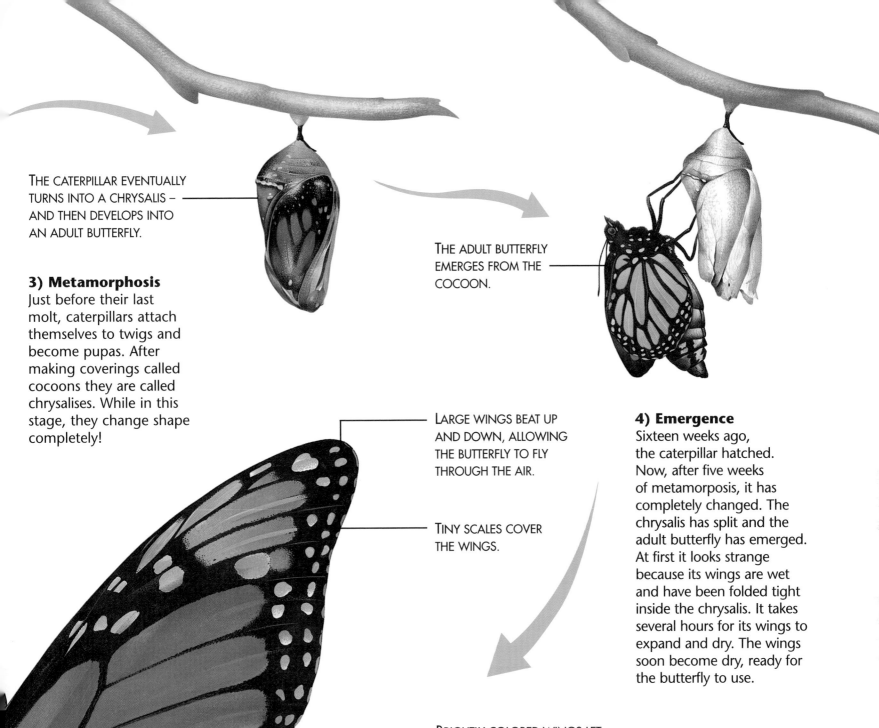

THE CATERPILLAR EVENTUALLY TURNS INTO A CHRYSALIS – AND THEN DEVELOPS INTO AN ADULT BUTTERFLY.

3) Metamorphosis
Just before their last molt, caterpillars attach themselves to twigs and become pupas. After making coverings called cocoons they are called chrysalises. While in this stage, they change shape completely!

THE ADULT BUTTERFLY EMERGES FROM THE COCOON.

LARGE WINGS BEAT UP AND DOWN, ALLOWING THE BUTTERFLY TO FLY THROUGH THE AIR.

TINY SCALES COVER THE WINGS.

4) Emergence
Sixteen weeks ago, the caterpillar hatched. Now, after five weeks of metamorposis, it has completely changed. The chrysalis has split and the adult butterfly has emerged. At first it looks strange because its wings are wet and have been folded tight inside the chrysalis. It takes several hours for its wings to expand and dry. The wings soon become dry, ready for the butterfly to use.

BRIGHTLY COLORED WINGS LET BUTTERFLIES COMMUNICATE WITH EACH OTHER AND WARN PREDATORS TO KEEP AWAY.

INTESTINE FOR DIGESTING NECTAR

THE ABDOMEN CONTAINS THE BODY'S MAIN ORGANS.

Migration
In autumn, monarch butterflies travel over 2,000 miles (3,200 km) south. They fly from Canada and the northern United States to Florida, Mexico, and California. When it is spring, the butterflies fly north, laying eggs along the way. Then they die.

A Frog's Life

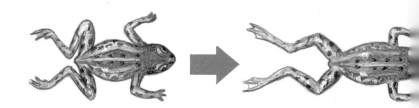

Colombian horned frogs, like all frogs, are coldblooded and have moist skin. They live in tropical American forests, hiding in the moss and dead leaves on the forest floor. These frogs are very aggressive and will even try to eat animals that are bigger than they are.

In general, frogs have large heads, bulging eyes, and wide mouths. The front legs are shorter than the strong back legs, which usually have extra long heels for hopping and swimming. Frogs need water to keep moist and to raise their young. They can breathe both on land and underwater. Animals that can breathe both on land and underwater are called amphibians.

Swimming
While bringing the front legs forward, the frog pulls its back legs toward its body. Then the front legs swing to the sides and the back legs shoot backward, pushing the frog forward.

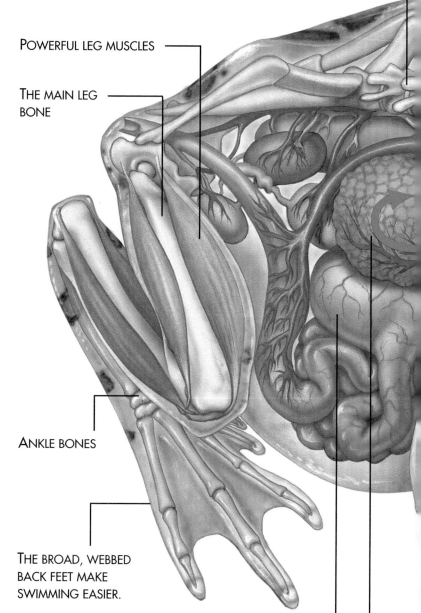

THE BACKBONE IS MADE UP OF SMALL BONES CALLED VERTEBRAE.

POWERFUL LEG MUSCLES

THE MAIN LEG BONE

ANKLE BONES

THE BROAD, WEBBED BACK FEET MAKE SWIMMING EASIER.

THE STOMACH

ON LAND, AIR IS BREATHED IN AND OUT OF THE LUNGS.

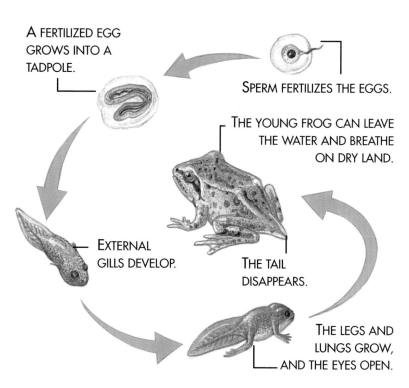

A FERTILIZED EGG GROWS INTO A TADPOLE.

SPERM FERTILIZES THE EGGS.

THE YOUNG FROG CAN LEAVE THE WATER AND BREATHE ON DRY LAND.

EXTERNAL GILLS DEVELOP.

THE TAIL DISAPPEARS.

THE LEGS AND LUNGS GROW, AND THE EYES OPEN.

Tadpole to frog
A female frog lays her eggs in water. The cluster of eggs is called her spawn. The spawn is fertilized by sperm from the male frog, and it then grows into balls of cells that develop into tadpoles. At first, tadpoles are blind and can only breathe underwater using external gills. Gradually, they change into frogs — a process called metamorphosis. Their eyes open, their legs grow, and their lungs develop. When they are completely developed, frogs can leave the water and breathe with their lungs.

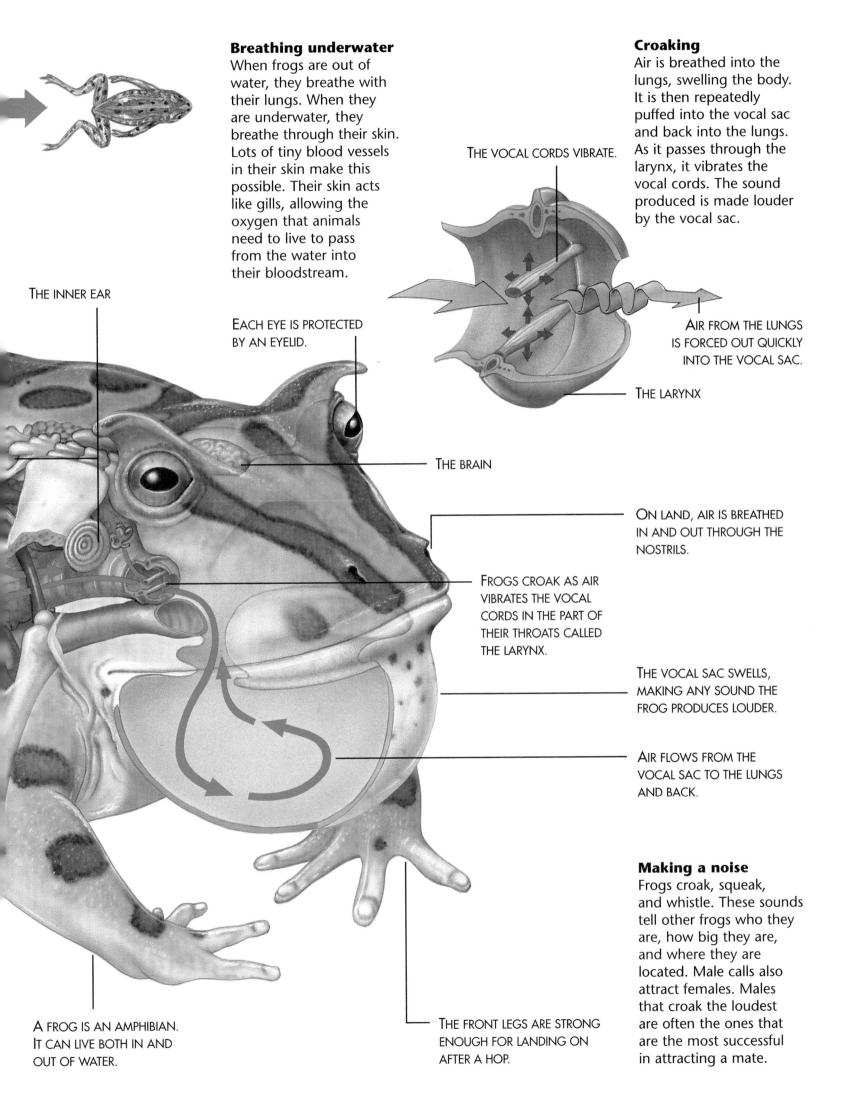

Breathing underwater
When frogs are out of water, they breathe with their lungs. When they are underwater, they breathe through their skin. Lots of tiny blood vessels in their skin make this possible. Their skin acts like gills, allowing the oxygen that animals need to live to pass from the water into their bloodstream.

Croaking
Air is breathed into the lungs, swelling the body. It is then repeatedly puffed into the vocal sac and back into the lungs. As it passes through the larynx, it vibrates the vocal cords. The sound produced is made louder by the vocal sac.

THE VOCAL CORDS VIBRATE.

THE INNER EAR

EACH EYE IS PROTECTED BY AN EYELID.

AIR FROM THE LUNGS IS FORCED OUT QUICKLY INTO THE VOCAL SAC.

THE LARYNX

THE BRAIN

ON LAND, AIR IS BREATHED IN AND OUT THROUGH THE NOSTRILS.

FROGS CROAK AS AIR VIBRATES THE VOCAL CORDS IN THE PART OF THEIR THROATS CALLED THE LARYNX.

THE VOCAL SAC SWELLS, MAKING ANY SOUND THE FROG PRODUCES LOUDER.

AIR FLOWS FROM THE VOCAL SAC TO THE LUNGS AND BACK.

Making a noise
Frogs croak, squeak, and whistle. These sounds tell other frogs who they are, how big they are, and where they are located. Male calls also attract females. Males that croak the loudest are often the ones that are the most successful in attracting a mate.

A FROG IS AN AMPHIBIAN. IT CAN LIVE BOTH IN AND OUT OF WATER.

THE FRONT LEGS ARE STRONG ENOUGH FOR LANDING ON AFTER A HOP.

Baby Mammals

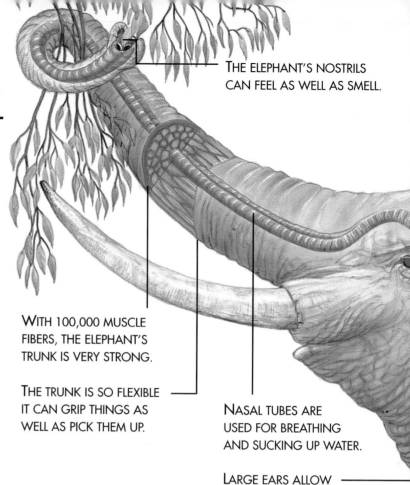

Mammals are warmblooded animals that feed their young with milk. Their milk is produced by the mother's mammary glands. Most mammals give birth to live young, which develop inside the mother's uterus. But even egg-laying mammals, such as the spiny anteater and duck-billed platypus, produce milk for their babies.

In mothers that give birth to live young, the babies are attached to the uterus by a tube called the umbilical cord. Through the cord they get food and oxygen, which they need to grow. Small mammals develop faster than large ones: a mouse takes about two weeks to develop, while an elephant takes twenty-two months. Humans develop in nine months. When mothers are ready to give birth, special chemicals in their bodies cause the uterus to push the baby out.

THE ELEPHANT'S NOSTRILS CAN FEEL AS WELL AS SMELL.

WITH 100,000 MUSCLE FIBERS, THE ELEPHANT'S TRUNK IS VERY STRONG.

THE TRUNK IS SO FLEXIBLE IT CAN GRIP THINGS AS WELL AS PICK THEM UP.

NASAL TUBES ARE USED FOR BREATHING AND SUCKING UP WATER.

LARGE EARS ALLOW EXTRA HEAT TO ESCAPE.

Marsupials

Marsupials are mammals that give birth to young that are not fully developed. The baby continues to develop in a pouch on the mother's belly. It drinks milk from the mother's nipples, which are in her pouch.

FERTILIZATION: A MALE SPERM CELL JOINS A FEMALE EGG.

A BALL OF CELLS FORMS AT THREE DAYS.

THIS IS THE ACTUAL SIZE OF A TWO-MONTH OLD ELEPHANT FETUS. ITS EYES ARE NOT YET FULLY DEVELOPED.

Fertilization and development

Every mammal starts out as a tiny egg in its mother's body. To become a baby, the egg must be joined by a sperm cell from the father. This process is called fertilization. The fertilized cell divides and grows into a ball of cells, which becomes attached to the wall of the female's uterus. The ball of cells starts to look like a baby animal as its head, body, and legs begin to grow. In this stage, the baby mammal is called a fetus.

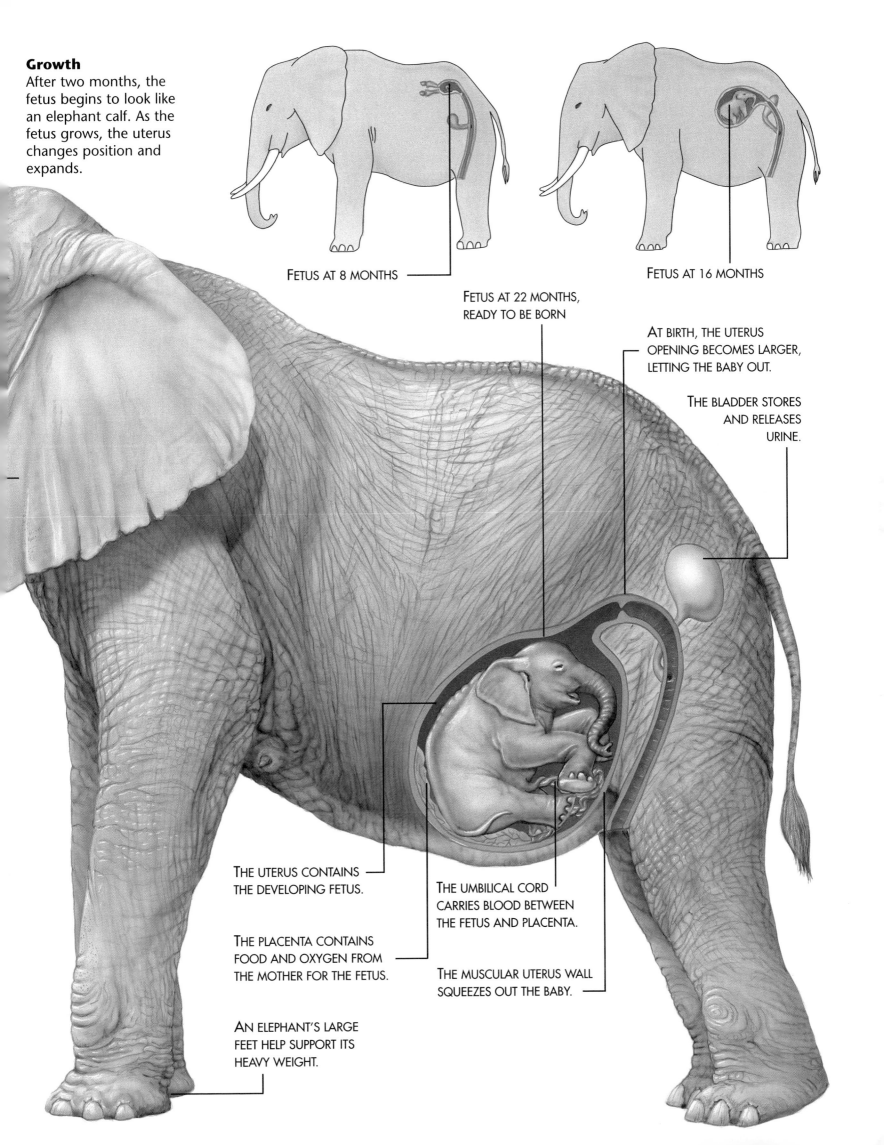

Growth
After two months, the fetus begins to look like an elephant calf. As the fetus grows, the uterus changes position and expands.

FETUS AT 8 MONTHS

FETUS AT 16 MONTHS

FETUS AT 22 MONTHS, READY TO BE BORN

AT BIRTH, THE UTERUS OPENING BECOMES LARGER, LETTING THE BABY OUT.

THE BLADDER STORES AND RELEASES URINE.

THE UTERUS CONTAINS THE DEVELOPING FETUS.

THE UMBILICAL CORD CARRIES BLOOD BETWEEN THE FETUS AND PLACENTA.

THE PLACENTA CONTAINS FOOD AND OXYGEN FROM THE MOTHER FOR THE FETUS.

THE MUSCULAR UTERUS WALL SQUEEZES OUT THE BABY.

AN ELEPHANT'S LARGE FEET HELP SUPPORT ITS HEAVY WEIGHT.

Hatching Eggs

Pheasants, like all birds, lay eggs. In fact, pheasants lay eight to fifteen eggs at a time. Eggs are strong, rounded structures that hold and protect the chicks while they develop. Each shell is made of strong, chalklike crystals and is lined with a tough membrane. The shell and membrane protect the chick from drying up while allowing it to receive oxygen from the air and let carbon dioxide out of the shell. Inside the shell, the chick rests in a soft, jellylike fluid. It receives nutrition from the yellow yolk. The outsides of the eggs are lightly colored and often flecked with brown so that they are not easily seen by predators. Nests help the mother bird protect her eggs and also make it possible for her to sit on them, keeping them warm.

Pheasant nests
It is important for the mother to hide her nest and eggs from foxes and weasels. To hide a nest, a small hole is dug into the ground under a hedge or layer of plants. Sometimes the hole is lined with leaves and stems. The pheasant's plain olive-brown-or gray-colored eggs can hardly be seen.

Embryo development
After the female and male bird have mated, the tiny fertilized egg cell divides and grows into more and more cells, forming a cluster of cells, called an embryo. As the embryo develops, the cells continue to divide, eventually forming the tissues and organs of the chick. Not all of the embryonic cells, however, become part of the developing chick. Some cells become blood vessels that carry food from the yolk to the chick. Other cells form a bag to hold waste that is excreted as the chick develops.

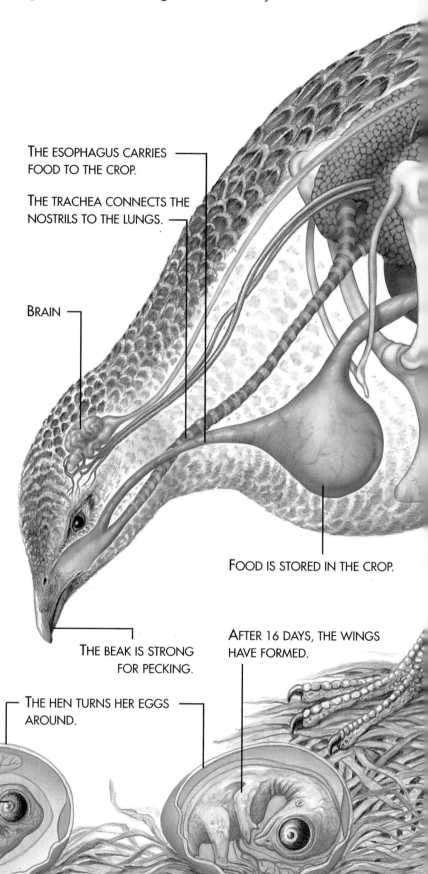

THE ESOPHAGUS CARRIES FOOD TO THE CROP.

THE TRACHEA CONNECTS THE NOSTRILS TO THE LUNGS.

BRAIN

FOOD IS STORED IN THE CROP.

THE BEAK IS STRONG FOR PECKING.

AFTER 16 DAYS, THE WINGS HAVE FORMED.

THE HEN TURNS HER EGGS AROUND.

TWO DAYS AFTER THE EGG HAS BEEN LAID, THE HEART PUMPS BLOOD TO THE YOLK SAC.

AFTER EIGHT DAYS, THE MAIN ORGANS AND THE CHICK'S LARGE EYES HAVE DEVELOPED.

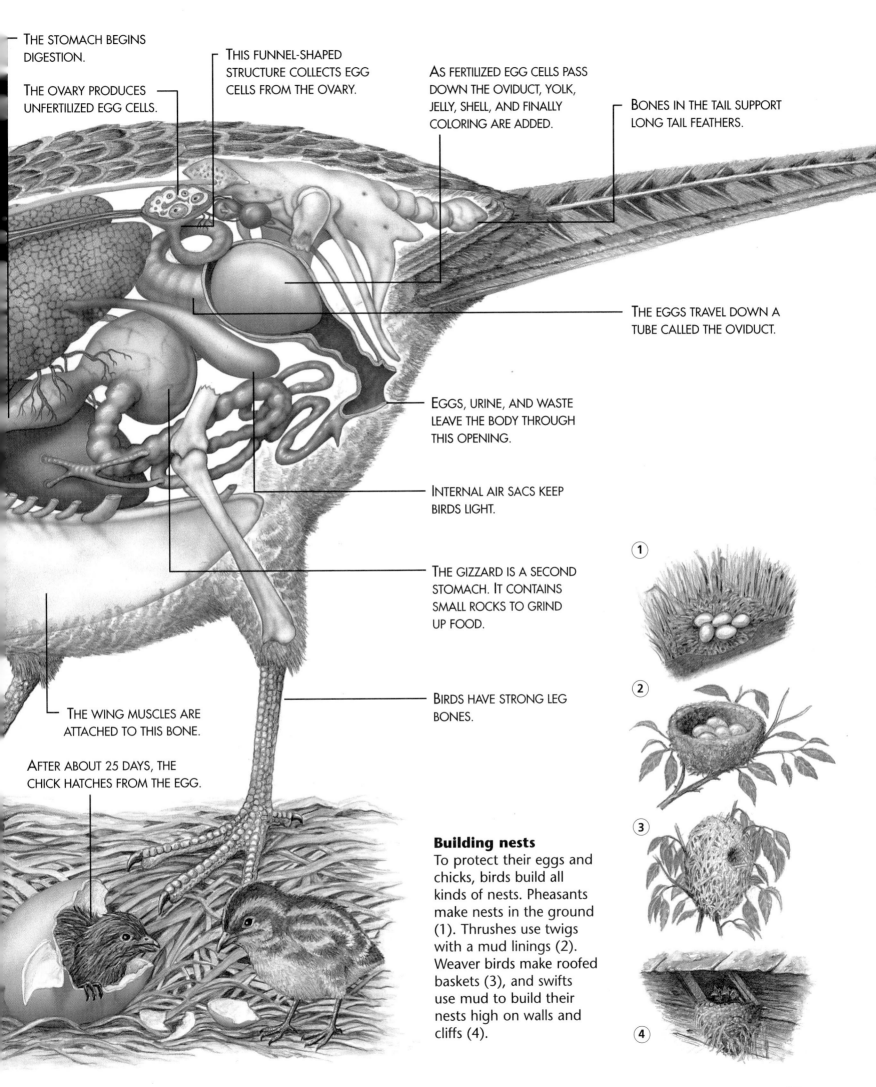

THE STOMACH BEGINS DIGESTION.

THE OVARY PRODUCES UNFERTILIZED EGG CELLS.

THIS FUNNEL-SHAPED STRUCTURE COLLECTS EGG CELLS FROM THE OVARY.

AS FERTILIZED EGG CELLS PASS DOWN THE OVIDUCT, YOLK, JELLY, SHELL, AND FINALLY COLORING ARE ADDED.

BONES IN THE TAIL SUPPORT LONG TAIL FEATHERS.

THE EGGS TRAVEL DOWN A TUBE CALLED THE OVIDUCT.

EGGS, URINE, AND WASTE LEAVE THE BODY THROUGH THIS OPENING.

INTERNAL AIR SACS KEEP BIRDS LIGHT.

THE GIZZARD IS A SECOND STOMACH. IT CONTAINS SMALL ROCKS TO GRIND UP FOOD.

BIRDS HAVE STRONG LEG BONES.

THE WING MUSCLES ARE ATTACHED TO THIS BONE.

AFTER ABOUT 25 DAYS, THE CHICK HATCHES FROM THE EGG.

Building nests

To protect their eggs and chicks, birds build all kinds of nests. Pheasants make nests in the ground (1). Thrushes use twigs with a mud linings (2). Weaver birds make roofed baskets (3), and swifts use mud to build their nests high on walls and cliffs (4).

1
2
3
4

Desert Animals

Camels mostly live in deserts. Their bodies are well-suited to survive the hot days, cold nights, wind-blown sand, and drought of the desert. Since they were first domesticated in Arabia nearly 4,000 years ago, camels have helped people live and travel in the desert. They can run as fast as 10 miles (16 km) per hour. Some camels are even bred especially for racing. Camels walk at about 2.5 miles (4 km) per hour and can travel up to 30 miles (50 km) each day. Camels can carry loads of up to 2,200 pounds (1,000 kg). Being able to travel well and carry heavy loads makes them ideal pack animals, which is why they are often called the "ships of the desert." They can also swim.

The camel's hump
Some camels have one hump; others have two. The one-humped Arabian camel, also called the dromedary, originally lived in Arabia. The two-humped Bactrian camel is found in Mongolia and Turkestan. Camels' humps are filled with fat. Once in the desert, away from food and water, they use the fat as a source of energy and water. When most of the fat has been used up, the hump shrivels and flops over. When camels eat and drink again, they store fat in their humps once more.

THE FAT-FILLED HUMP

SOFT, WOOLLY HAIR KEEPS CAMELS FROM COOLING DOWN TOO QUICKLY IN THE COLD DESERT NIGHT.

THE SKIN HAS FEW SWEAT GLANDS TO AVOID TOO MUCH WATER LOSS.

A LONG NECK ENABLES THE CAMEL TO TAKE A DRINK WITHOUT KNEELING DOWN.

SMALL, HAIRY EARS KEEP OUT SAND.

LONG EYELASHES AND BIG EYELIDS PROTECT EYES FROM THE SUN AND FLYING SAND.

NOSTRILS CAN CLOSE TO KEEP OUT THE SAND.

SALIVARY GLANDS HELP DIGEST FOOD.

WITH STRONG TEETH AND LIPS, CAMELS CAN EAT TOUGH PLANTS. SALTY PLANTS HELP THEM RETAIN WATER.

TOUGH PADS OF SKIN PROTECT THE KNEES AND CHEST WHEN THE CAMEL RESTS ITS WEIGHT ON THEM.

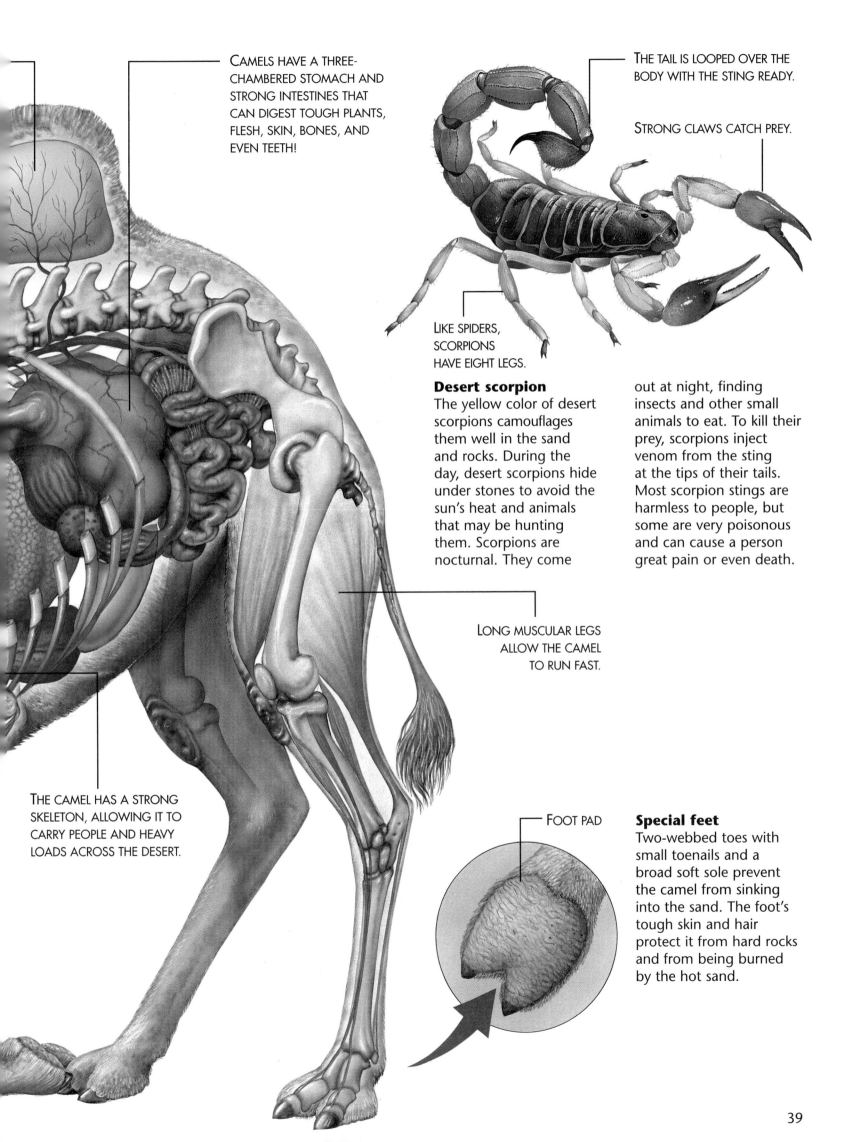

CAMELS HAVE A THREE-CHAMBERED STOMACH AND STRONG INTESTINES THAT CAN DIGEST TOUGH PLANTS, FLESH, SKIN, BONES, AND EVEN TEETH!

THE TAIL IS LOOPED OVER THE BODY WITH THE STING READY.

STRONG CLAWS CATCH PREY.

LIKE SPIDERS, SCORPIONS HAVE EIGHT LEGS.

Desert scorpion

The yellow color of desert scorpions camouflages them well in the sand and rocks. During the day, desert scorpions hide under stones to avoid the sun's heat and animals that may be hunting them. Scorpions are nocturnal. They come out at night, finding insects and other small animals to eat. To kill their prey, scorpions inject venom from the sting at the tips of their tails. Most scorpion stings are harmless to people, but some are very poisonous and can cause a person great pain or even death.

LONG MUSCULAR LEGS ALLOW THE CAMEL TO RUN FAST.

THE CAMEL HAS A STRONG SKELETON, ALLOWING IT TO CARRY PEOPLE AND HEAVY LOADS ACROSS THE DESERT.

FOOT PAD

Special feet

Two-webbed toes with small toenails and a broad soft sole prevent the camel from sinking into the sand. The foot's tough skin and hair protect it from hard rocks and from being burned by the hot sand.

Arctic Animals

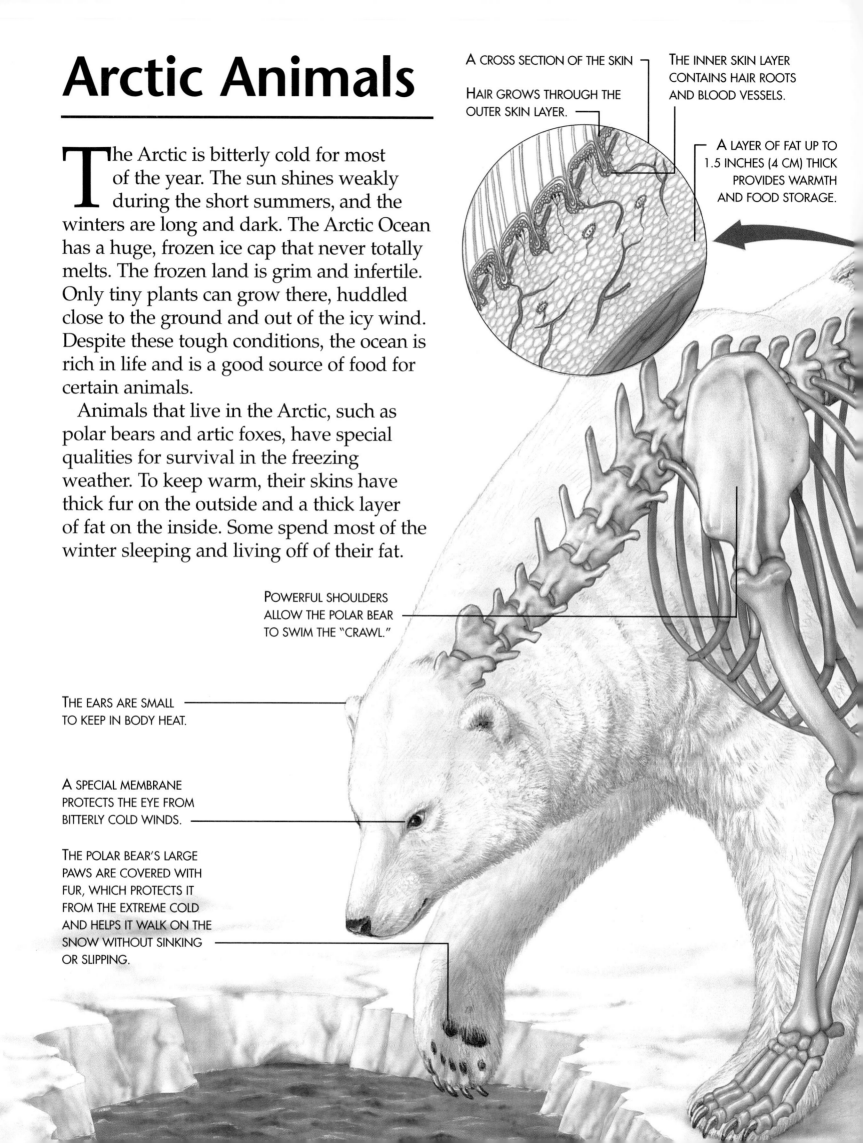

The Arctic is bitterly cold for most of the year. The sun shines weakly during the short summers, and the winters are long and dark. The Arctic Ocean has a huge, frozen ice cap that never totally melts. The frozen land is grim and infertile. Only tiny plants can grow there, huddled close to the ground and out of the icy wind. Despite these tough conditions, the ocean is rich in life and is a good source of food for certain animals.

Animals that live in the Arctic, such as polar bears and artic foxes, have special qualities for survival in the freezing weather. To keep warm, their skins have thick fur on the outside and a thick layer of fat on the inside. Some spend most of the winter sleeping and living off of their fat.

A CROSS SECTION OF THE SKIN

HAIR GROWS THROUGH THE OUTER SKIN LAYER.

THE INNER SKIN LAYER CONTAINS HAIR ROOTS AND BLOOD VESSELS.

A LAYER OF FAT UP TO 1.5 INCHES (4 CM) THICK PROVIDES WARMTH AND FOOD STORAGE.

POWERFUL SHOULDERS ALLOW THE POLAR BEAR TO SWIM THE "CRAWL."

THE EARS ARE SMALL TO KEEP IN BODY HEAT.

A SPECIAL MEMBRANE PROTECTS THE EYE FROM BITTERLY COLD WINDS.

THE POLAR BEAR'S LARGE PAWS ARE COVERED WITH FUR, WHICH PROTECTS IT FROM THE EXTREME COLD AND HELPS IT WALK ON THE SNOW WITHOUT SINKING OR SLIPPING.

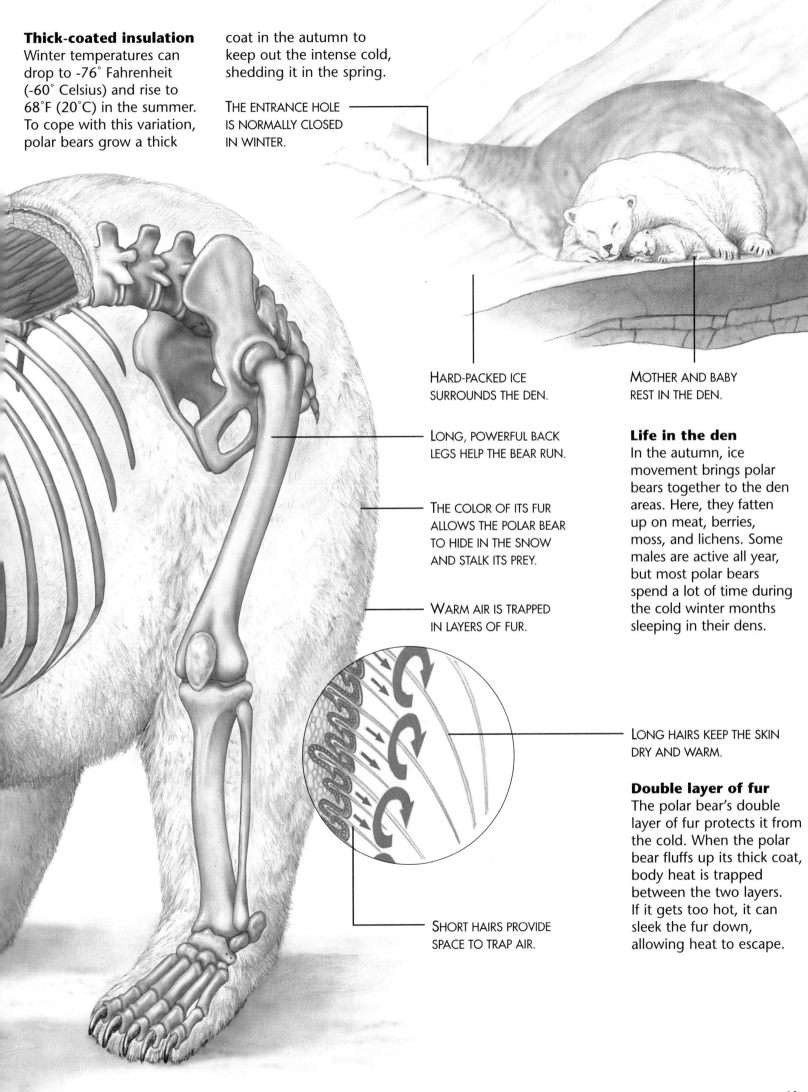

Thick-coated insulation
Winter temperatures can drop to -76° Fahrenheit (-60° Celsius) and rise to 68°F (20°C) in the summer. To cope with this variation, polar bears grow a thick coat in the autumn to keep out the intense cold, shedding it in the spring.

THE ENTRANCE HOLE IS NORMALLY CLOSED IN WINTER.

HARD-PACKED ICE SURROUNDS THE DEN.

MOTHER AND BABY REST IN THE DEN.

LONG, POWERFUL BACK LEGS HELP THE BEAR RUN.

THE COLOR OF ITS FUR ALLOWS THE POLAR BEAR TO HIDE IN THE SNOW AND STALK ITS PREY.

WARM AIR IS TRAPPED IN LAYERS OF FUR.

Life in the den
In the autumn, ice movement brings polar bears together to the den areas. Here, they fatten up on meat, berries, moss, and lichens. Some males are active all year, but most polar bears spend a lot of time during the cold winter months sleeping in their dens.

LONG HAIRS KEEP THE SKIN DRY AND WARM.

Double layer of fur
The polar bear's double layer of fur protects it from the cold. When the polar bear fluffs up its thick coat, body heat is trapped between the two layers. If it gets too hot, it can sleek the fur down, allowing heat to escape.

SHORT HAIRS PROVIDE SPACE TO TRAP AIR.

Primates

Primates are mammals that have very large brains. The thinking part of their brains is especially big, making them very intelligent. Monkeys, chimpanzees, lemurs, and humans are all primates. Most primates live in warmer climates, except for humans, who live in most parts of the world.

Primates can be very big. For example, gorillas can weigh up to 400 pounds (180 kg). The tiny mouse lemur weighs only 1.8 ounces (50 grams). Nearly all primates are good at climbing trees. To help them do this, they have special eyes, hands, and feet. Many also have long tails. To communicate, primates use many different sounds. Of all the primates, humans make the largest assortment of sounds.

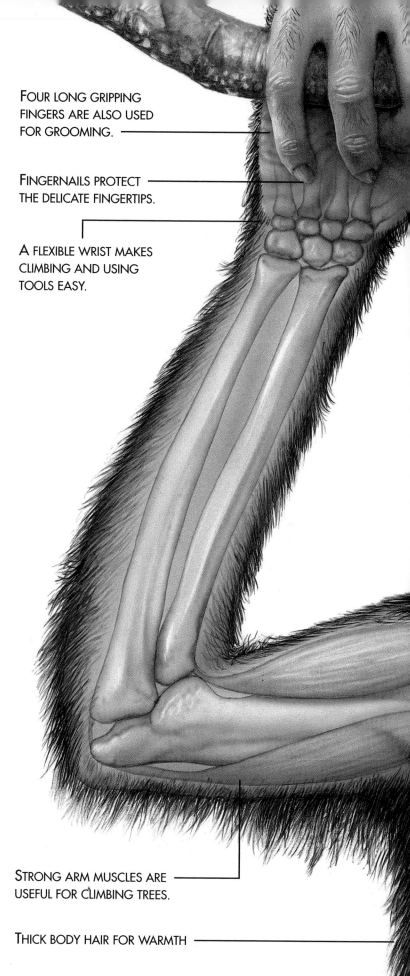

FOUR LONG GRIPPING FINGERS ARE ALSO USED FOR GROOMING.

FINGERNAILS PROTECT THE DELICATE FINGERTIPS.

A FLEXIBLE WRIST MAKES CLIMBING AND USING TOOLS EASY.

STRONG ARM MUSCLES ARE USEFUL FOR CLIMBING TREES.

THICK BODY HAIR FOR WARMTH

①

②

③

④

Chimp expressions
Some primates, such as chimpanzees, show their emotions through facial expressions. These include the following: (1) mouth closed when attacking – "You've made me angry"; (2) mouth open to show all the teeth – "I'm scared"; (3) mouth open, with the bottom teeth showing – "Let's play"; (4) lips pushed forward – "Give it to me."

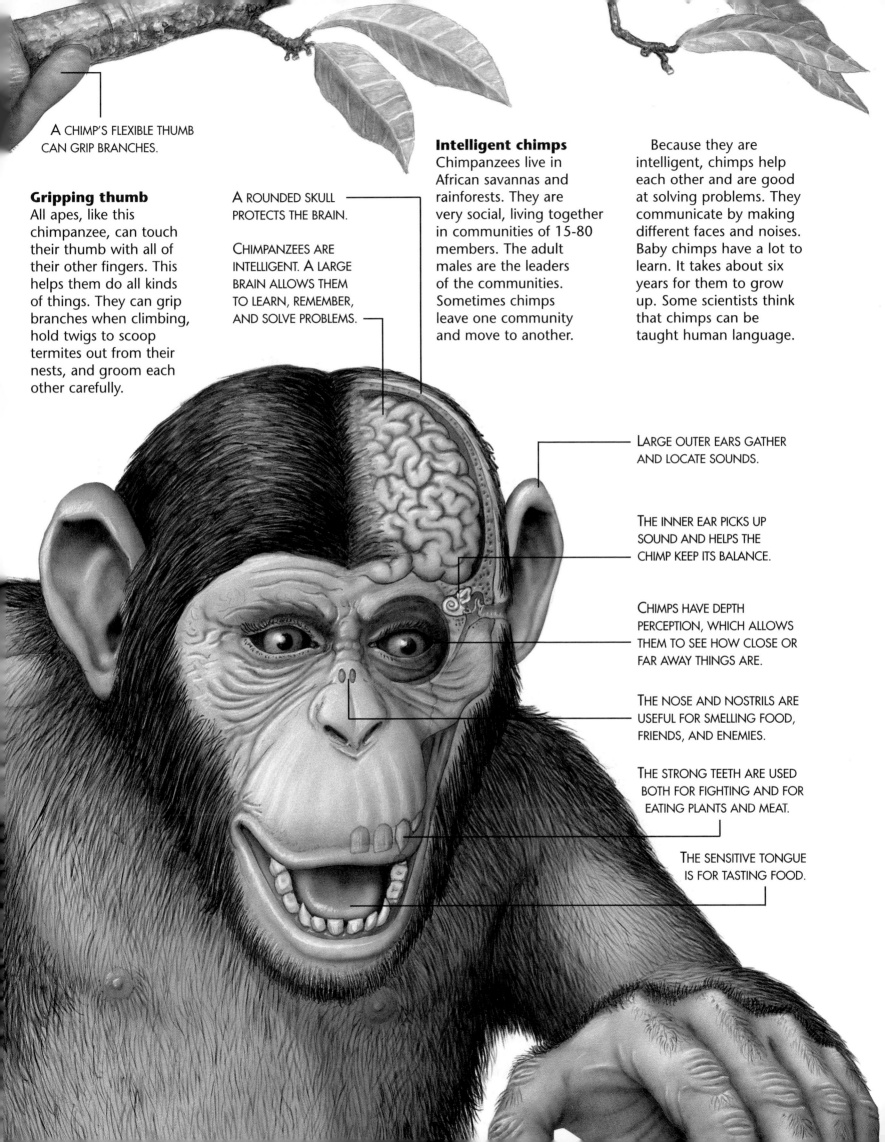

A CHIMP'S FLEXIBLE THUMB CAN GRIP BRANCHES.

Gripping thumb
All apes, like this chimpanzee, can touch their thumb with all of their other fingers. This helps them do all kinds of things. They can grip branches when climbing, hold twigs to scoop termites out from their nests, and groom each other carefully.

A ROUNDED SKULL PROTECTS THE BRAIN.

CHIMPANZEES ARE INTELLIGENT. A LARGE BRAIN ALLOWS THEM TO LEARN, REMEMBER, AND SOLVE PROBLEMS.

Intelligent chimps
Chimpanzees live in African savannas and rainforests. They are very social, living together in communities of 15-80 members. The adult males are the leaders of the communities. Sometimes chimps leave one community and move to another.

Because they are intelligent, chimps help each other and are good at solving problems. They communicate by making different faces and noises. Baby chimps have a lot to learn. It takes about six years for them to grow up. Some scientists think that chimps can be taught human language.

LARGE OUTER EARS GATHER AND LOCATE SOUNDS.

THE INNER EAR PICKS UP SOUND AND HELPS THE CHIMP KEEP ITS BALANCE.

CHIMPS HAVE DEPTH PERCEPTION, WHICH ALLOWS THEM TO SEE HOW CLOSE OR FAR AWAY THINGS ARE.

THE NOSE AND NOSTRILS ARE USEFUL FOR SMELLING FOOD, FRIENDS, AND ENEMIES.

THE STRONG TEETH ARE USED BOTH FOR FIGHTING AND FOR EATING PLANTS AND MEAT.

THE SENSITIVE TONGUE IS FOR TASTING FOOD.

Community Life

Millions of termites live together in communities called colonies. Each termite does a specific job. For example, some termites gather food, some look after the young, and others guard the colony against enemy attack. Termites are social insects, and each individual works toward the good of the whole colony. In such a large community, good communication is important. The termites need to respond to problems as soon as they come up. One way termites communicate is by releasing special chemicals for other termites to smell.

Most termites are pale and have soft bodies, so they need to avoid dry air and sunlight. They hide inside their nests and burrows and only come out at night, if at all. Some termites use soil to make very complicated nests. Others carve simple structures inside rotting wood.

Soldiers

Ants are termites' main enemies. The soldier termites defend the colony from ant attack using their special jaws. Some termites bite, while others use their jaws to spray a sticky glue at the attacker. Soldier termites are not able to feed themselves; they must be fed by the worker termites.

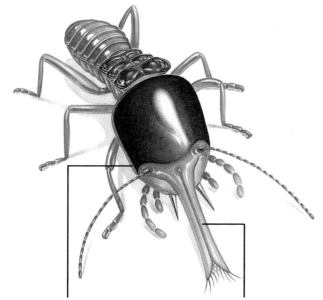

POWERFUL JAW MUSCLES ARE IN THE LARGE HEAD.

GLUE IS SPRAYED OUT THROUGH THIS TUBE.

Air circulation

When millions of termites live together, they need plenty of fresh air to breathe. They also need to keep the air cool, so termites build their nest so the air moves through it, keeping it fresh and cool. This circulating air also allows the chemical scents that they use for communication to carry through the colony.

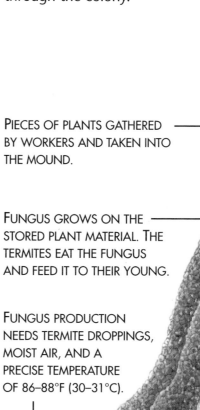

HOT STALE AIR RISES AND ESCAPES THROUGH THE CHIMNEYS.

POROUS CHIMNEY MATERIAL DRAWS IN FRESH AIR AND RELEASES THE STALE AIR.

PIECES OF PLANTS GATHERED BY WORKERS AND TAKEN INTO THE MOUND.

FUNGUS GROWS ON THE STORED PLANT MATERIAL. THE TERMITES EAT THE FUNGUS AND FEED IT TO THEIR YOUNG.

FUNGUS PRODUCTION NEEDS TERMITE DROPPINGS, MOIST AIR, AND A PRECISE TEMPERATURE OF 86–88°F (30–31°C).

UNDERGROUND CELLARS COOL THE AIR AND GIVE THE NEST MOISTURE.

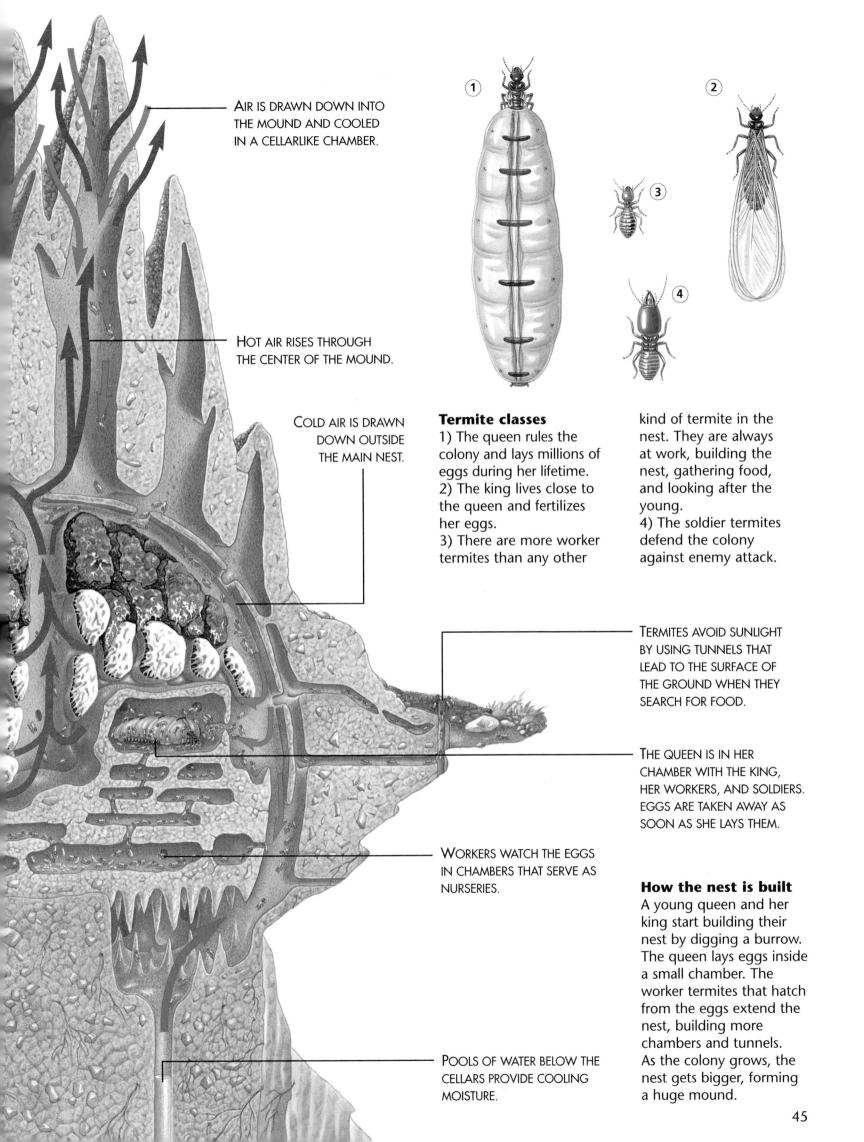

AIR IS DRAWN DOWN INTO THE MOUND AND COOLED IN A CELLARLIKE CHAMBER.

HOT AIR RISES THROUGH THE CENTER OF THE MOUND.

COLD AIR IS DRAWN DOWN OUTSIDE THE MAIN NEST.

Termite classes

1) The queen rules the colony and lays millions of eggs during her lifetime.
2) The king lives close to the queen and fertilizes her eggs.
3) There are more worker termites than any other kind of termite in the nest. They are always at work, building the nest, gathering food, and looking after the young.
4) The soldier termites defend the colony against enemy attack.

TERMITES AVOID SUNLIGHT BY USING TUNNELS THAT LEAD TO THE SURFACE OF THE GROUND WHEN THEY SEARCH FOR FOOD.

THE QUEEN IS IN HER CHAMBER WITH THE KING, HER WORKERS, AND SOLDIERS. EGGS ARE TAKEN AWAY AS SOON AS SHE LAYS THEM.

WORKERS WATCH THE EGGS IN CHAMBERS THAT SERVE AS NURSERIES.

How the nest is built

A young queen and her king start building their nest by digging a burrow. The queen lays eggs inside a small chamber. The worker termites that hatch from the eggs extend the nest, building more chambers and tunnels. As the colony grows, the nest gets bigger, forming a huge mound.

POOLS OF WATER BELOW THE CELLARS PROVIDE COOLING MOISTURE.

Glossary

algae: plantlike organisms that live in water and do not have roots, stems, and leaves.

amphibians: cold-blooded animals, such as frogs, that can breathe both on land and in water.

antennae: light, thin, movable "feelers" on the heads of most insects.

Arctic: the region or area of land that surrounds the North Pole.

baleen: hard, bony plates in certain whales' mouths. The baleen trap food for the whale to eat.

barb: a sharp point that is designed to catch things, such as the point on a fishhook.

cloven hoof: a hoof that is split, having two toes. Cows, sheep, deer, and goats have cloven hooves.

coral: a hard material that is made from the skeletons of sea polyps. The skeletons fuse together to create large structures called reefs.

cud: food that has been swallowed by an animal and then brought back up to the mouth for chewing. Cows, sheep, and deer chew cud.

digest: to break down food in the stomach.

domesticate: to train certain animals so they can live with humans as pets or work animals.

echolocation: a method by which bats and marine animals use sound and hearing to guide themselves in the dark.

embryo: a human or animal in the earliest growth stage inside its mother's body or egg.

esophagus: the tube that connects the stomach and the throat.

fangs: the sharp "teeth" of snakes, often used to inject poison.

fetus: an unborn or unhatched animal, after it has developed the features of its species.

gills: organs that absorb oxygen from water.

herbivore: an animal that eats only plants.

krill: tiny, shrimplike ocean creatures.

maim: to cripple a body part.

marine animals: animals that live in the sea.

metamorphosis: the process of changing from one shape to another. For example, the process by which a caterpillar changes into a butterfly.

nocturnal: active at night.

placenta: the organ in female animals that provides the growing fetus with what it needs to live.

polyps: tube-shaped body parts of some invertebrates. Different kinds of polyps do different jobs for the animal.

predators: animals that hunt and eat other animals.

prey: animals that are hunted and eaten by other animals.

quills: the sharp, hollow spines that protect porcupines and hedgehogs.

retract: to pull back.

rudder: a thin, hinged wood or metal plate used for steering ships. Rudders are attached to the back of the ship.

ruminants: animals that have a rumen, which is the part of a stomach that softens food into cud.

saliva: the fluid secreted into the the mouth from the salivary glands that moistens the mouth, makes food more easily chewable, and begins the digestion of starches.

sea anemones: animals that live in the sea that have flexible tentacles and tube-shaped bodies.

species: a group of animals or plants that have certain features in common.

uterus: the structure in the female body that holds the developing baby before it is born.

venom: the poisonous fluid that some animals inject into others by biting or stinging.

victim: a person or animal that has been hurt or killed by the action of another or by accident.

waste: material that is not usable by the body and must be expelled.

More Books to Read

3-D Bees and Micro Fleas: See Insects Magnified Up to 500,000 Times! Eye-to-Eye Books (series). Shar Levine, Dr. Elaine Humphrey, Leslie Johnstone (Somerville House)

The Amazing Book of Bird Records: The Largest, the Smallest, the Fastest, and Many More. Amazing Animal Records (series). Samuel G. Woods (Blackbirch Marketing)

Amazing Mammals. Ranger Rick's Naturescope (series). National Wildlife Federation, Sandra Stotksy (Chelsea House)

Animal Fact File: Head-to-Tail Profiles of More Than 90 Mammals. Dr. Tony Hare (Facts on File)

The Beginner's Guide to Animal Autopsy: The Hands-In Approach to Zoology. Steve Parker (Copper Beech Books)

Beneath the Oceans. Worldwise (series). Penny Clarke (Franklin Watts)

Fantastic Facts: Insects. Jen Green (Hermes House)

Insects. National Audubon Society First Field Guides (series). Christina Wilsdon (Scholastic Trade)

The Snake Scientist. Sy Montgomery (Houghton Mifflin)

Tough Terminators: Nature's Most Amazing Animals. It's Nature! (series). Sneed B. Collard III (Creative Publishing International)

Whales, Dolphins, and Porpoises. DK Handbooks (series). Mark Carwardine (DK Publishing)

Videos

Favorite Animals. (National Geographic)

In the Company of Whales. (Discovery Communication)

Wild Kingdom: New Animal World Collection. (Madacy Entertainment)

Zoo Life with Jack Hanna: Amazing Animals. (Time-Life Video)

Web Sites

Animals of the World
   www.kidscom.com/orakc/Games/Animalgame/ animalright.html

Extreme Science: World Records of the Animal Kingdom
   extremescience.com/creatport.htm

Kids' Planet
   www.kidsplanet.org/

King Cobra
   www.nationalgeographic.com/kingcobra/

The Life of Birds
   www.pbs.org/lifeofbirds/home/

SeaWorld/Busch Gardens: Animal Bytes
   www.seaworld.org/animal_bytes/animal_ bytes.html

U.S. Fish and Wildlife Service: Kids Corner
   endangered.fws.gov/kids/

Wildlife Conservation Society: Kids Go Wild
   www.kidsgowild.com

Some web sites stay current longer than others. For further web sites, use your search engines to locate the following topics: *butterflies, gastropods, invertebrates, mollusks, primates, reptiles,* and *whales.*

Index